around the **world**

in 65 recipes

A delicious collection of low Point recipes

SIMON & SCHUSTER
A VIACOM COMPANY

Sue Ashworth

First published in Great Britain by Simon & Schuster UK Ltd, 2003
A Viacom Company

Simon & Schuster UK Ltd
Africa House
64–78 Kingsway
London
WC2B 6AH

Photography by Iain Bagwell
Styling by Rachel Jukes
Food preparation by Penny Stephens

Design by Jane Humphrey
Typesetting by Stylize Digital Artwork
Printed and bound in China

Weight Watchers Publications Manager: Corrina Griffin
Weight Watchers Publications Executives: Lucy Davidson,
Mandy Spittle
Weight Watchers Publications Assistant: Nina Bhogal

A CIP catalogue for this book is available from the British Library

ISBN 0743239024

Pictured on the front cover: Chicken Tikka Masala, page 25

Pictured on the back cover: Tiramisu with Strawberries, page 57

Raw Eggs: Only the freshest eggs should be used. Pregnant
women, the elderly and children should avoid recipes with
eggs which are not fully cooked or raw.

All fruits, vegetables and eggs are medium size unless otherwise
stated.

Recipe timings are approximate and meant to be guidelines.
Please note that the preparation time includes all the steps
up to and following the main cooking time(s).

You'll find this easy to read logo on every recipe
throughout the book. The logo represents the
number of Points per serving each recipe contains.
The easy to use Points system is designed to help
you eat what you want, when you want – as long
as you stay within your Points allowance – giving
you the freedom to enjoy the food you love.

(v) This symbol denotes a vegetarian recipe and
assumes vegetarian cheese and free range eggs
are used. Virtually fat free fromage frais and low
fat crème fraîche may contain traces of gelatine
so they are not always vegetarian: please check
the labels.

(Vg) This symbol denotes a vegan dish.

contents

4 Introduction

7 Soups & Starters

14 Meals for One or Two

23 Meat & Poultry

32 Vegetarian Main Courses

42 Fish Main Courses

53 Desserts

64 Index

fabulous food from around the world

Take your tastebuds on a trip around the world

with this wonderful Weight Watchers cookbook,

designed to keep you stepping in the right

direction on your journey to becoming the real

you. If you've already reached your desired weight,

then this cookbook will keep you inspired to stay

on track – keeping fit, eating healthily, staying

slim and being happy.

Some of you may be quite new to cooking, and many of you will have had years of experience. Either way, if you choose a recipe that you like the sound of, you can be sure that when you cook it, it's going to taste good. Don't ever think that because a recipe is low in Points, it is also lacking flavour – nothing could be further from the truth in this cookbook. With fresh, flavourful ingredients these recipes are usually tastier than the high fat version.

If you're following the Weight Watchers **Time To Eat**™ Programme, then make a little time to cook too. It's true that most of us lead very busy lifestyles these days – juggling work, family commitments and running the home, yet it's no reason to abandon a healthy lifestyle. It's so important to keep healthy by eating a sensible, balanced diet and taking plenty of exercise in order to cope with the everyday demands on our time.

With time in mind, many of these recipes have been created for busy people to cook and enjoy. Every recipe gives timings for preparation and cooking, so you can check these before you begin. No matter how little time you have, it's not a good idea to resort to fast food and ready meals as they are usually less healthy and more expensive than home made food – and they don't taste as good. Surely it's not too much trouble to rustle up a meal for your family and friends, or your partner – and very importantly – yourself. After all, who is going to look after your health if you don't?

I hope that you enjoy globetrotting through the pages of this cookbook, and I sincerely hope that when you cook them you – and whoever else may be joining you – enjoys eating them too.

Happy cooking! Sue Ashworth.

Thai Spring Rolls: Deliciously refreshing and just ½ a Point each.

soups & starters

Dive into this chapter for some all time favourite recipes from around the world. There are five fabulous low Point soups to choose from, giving you a taste of Italy, Spain, France, China and the USA, and lots of delicious starters, including finger licking sticky ribs and succulent garlic prawns.

THAI SPRING ROLLS

4¹⁄₂ Points per recipe

Ⓥ Ⓥⱺ *if following variation*
Makes 8
Preparation time: 15 minutes
Calories per pancake: 55
Freezing: not recommended

These spring rolls are light, tasty and so low in Points – a far cry from the deep fried restaurant versions.

50 g pack (8 pancakes) of rice flour pancakes for spring rolls
50 g (1³⁄₄ oz) fresh beansprouts
2 spring onions, sliced finely
¹⁄₂ red pepper, de-seeded and sliced very finely
2–3 Chinese leaves or Cos lettuce leaves, shredded finely
50 g (1³⁄₄ oz) cooked small prawns, defrosted if frozen

1 teaspoon seasoned rice vinegar or white wine vinegar
2 teaspoons Thai fish sauce or soy sauce
salt and freshly ground black pepper
4 tablespoons sweet chilli sauce, to serve

1 First prepare the rice flour pancakes. Take two clean tea towels, run them under the cold tap and wring them out. Spread one out on a worktop, lay the spring roll pancakes on top, and then cover them with the second damp tea towel. Leave for 1–2 minutes until the pancakes are soft and pliable.
2 Put all the vegetables and the prawns into a bowl, and add the rice vinegar or white wine vinegar and the fish sauce or soy sauce. Season with a little salt and pepper, and then toss everything together.

3 Place an equal amount of the vegetable and prawn filling down the centre of each pancake. Fold in the sides, and then roll up each pancake to enclose the filling.
4 Cover and chill the spring rolls until ready to serve. Serve chilled, accompanied by the sweet chilli sauce for dipping.

Top tip For the spring roll pancakes, it's a good idea to check the pack instructions on preparation as individual brands may differ slightly.

Variation For a vegetarian alternative, omit the prawns and make sure that you use soy sauce, not fish sauce. If you like, add a few raw sliced button mushrooms in step two.

Gazpacho: Loads of flavour but No Points!

GAZPACHO

1 Point per recipe

(V) (Vg) Serves 6

Preparation time: 20 minutes +
3–4 hours chilling

Calories per serving: 50

Freezing: recommended

Serve this tomato based, chilled
Spanish soup in the summer as a
cool and refreshing No Point starter.

1 bunch of spring onions, chopped
roughly

4 ripe tomatoes, peeled and chopped
roughly

1/2 cucumber, chopped roughly

1 small green pepper, de-seeded and
chopped roughly

1 garlic clove, crushed

2 tablespoons chopped fresh flat leaf
parsley or mint

400 g can of chopped tomatoes

300 ml (10 fl oz) tomato juice, chilled

3 tablespoons red wine vinegar

1 teaspoon caster sugar

300 ml (10 fl oz) chilled water

salt and freshly ground black pepper

1 tablespoon each of finely chopped
red onion, cucumber, red pepper and
tomatoes, to garnish

1 Place all the ingredients, apart
from the garnishes, in a blender or
food processor and liquidise until
smooth. Do this in batches, if
necessary.

2 Strain the soup through a sieve,
using the back of a wooden spoon
to push it through, extracting as
much liquid as possible from the
ingredients. Cover and chill until icy
cold for 3–4 hours, or overnight if
preferred.

3 Taste the soup and check the
seasoning, adding salt and pepper
according to taste. Ladle the soup
into six bowls and top with the
garnishes.

Top tip An easy way to peel tomatoes
is to put them into a bowl and cover
them with boiling water. Leave for
15–20 seconds, and then remove
from the water and slip off their
skins.

Variation If you're not keen on
peppers, leave them out and use
another two tomatoes instead.

SEAFOOD CHOWDER

10 Points per recipe

Serves 4

Preparation time: 15 minutes

Cooking time: 30 minutes

Calories per serving: 205

Freezing: recommended

Chowders are thick, chunky soups
with a creamy base – very popular
in the USA.

low fat cooking spray

1 onion, chopped finely

250 g (9 oz) potatoes, peeled and diced

2 vegetable stock cubes, dissolved in
850 ml (1 1/2 pints) boiling water

50 g (1 3/4 oz) frozen peas

200 g (7 oz) smoked haddock, skinned,
boned and cut into chunks

100 g (3 1/2 oz) cooked peeled prawns,
defrosted if frozen

300 ml (10 fl oz) skimmed milk

2 tablespoons chopped fresh parsley

2 tablespoons cornflour, blended with
5 tablespoons cold water

salt and freshly ground black pepper

1 Lightly spray a large saucepan with
low fat cooking spray and sauté the
onion for 5 minutes, until softened.

2 Add the potatoes and stock to
the saucepan. Heat, then cover and
simmer gently for about 15 minutes,
until the potatoes are tender.

3 Add the peas, haddock, prawns,
milk and half the parsley. Cook over
a low heat for about 5 minutes, until
the fish is opaque.

4 Add the blended cornflour to the
saucepan and heat, stirring until
thickened. Season, then serve in
four warmed bowls, sprinkled with
the remaining parsley.

Seafood Chowder:
A meal in itself for
only 2½ Points.

Sticky Ribs:
Finger licking
sticky ribs for
an incredible
5½ Points.

STICKY RIBS

5½ POINTS

22 Points per recipe
Serves 4
Preparation time: 10 minutes
Cooking time: 1 hour
Calories per serving: 355
Freezing: not recommended

Chinese style pork spare ribs make
a very tasty starter – or you could
serve them as a main meal with 4
tablespoons of boiled rice, adding
an extra 3 Points per serving.

500 g (1 lb 2 oz) pork spare ribs
4 tablespoons tomato purée
2 tablespoons rice or cider vinegar
2 tablespoons soy sauce
2 tablespoons hoisin sauce
1 teaspoon Chinese five spice powder
2 teaspoons light or dark muscovado
sugar
salt and freshly ground black pepper

To serve
1 tablespoon chopped fresh coriander
or parsley
2 spring onions, sliced finely

1 Preheat the oven to Gas Mark 6/
200°C/fan oven 180°C.
2 Put the spare ribs into a large
roasting pan.
3 In a bowl, mix together the tomato
purée, rice or cider vinegar, soy

sauce, hoisin sauce, five spice
powder and sugar. Season with salt
and pepper and brush this mixture
generously over the ribs to glaze
them.
4 Roast the ribs for 30 minutes,
then baste them again with the
leftover glazing mixture, adding any
remaining mixture to the roasting
pan. Roast the ribs for a further
20–25 minutes.
5 Serve the ribs, sprinkled with the
chopped coriander or parsley and
sliced spring onions.

Variations Substitute oyster sauce
for the hoisin sauce if you prefer.
The Points will be reduced to 5 per
serving. For extra bite, add a teaspoon
or two of hot chilli sauce to the
glaze mixture. The Points will remain
the same.

CHICKEN NOODLE SOUP

1½ POINTS

5½ Points per recipe
Serves 4
Preparation and cooking time:
35 minutes
Calories per serving: 125
Freezing: recommended

A bowlful of this tasty low Point
soup with its authentic Chinese
flavour is wonderfully filling and
enjoyable.

2 chicken stock cubes, dissolved in
850 ml (1½ pints) boiling water
1 bunch of spring onions, shredded
into fine strips
1 small leek, shredded into fine strips

½ teaspoon Chinese five spice powder
1 teaspoon finely grated fresh root
ginger or ¼ teaspoon ground ginger
2 tablespoons light soy sauce
50 g (1¾ oz) thread egg noodles
50 g (1¾ oz) sweetcorn, defrosted
if frozen
50 g (1¾ oz) cooked chicken, shredded
into fine strips
1 tablespoon cornflour, blended with
3 tablespoons cold water
salt and freshly ground black pepper

1 Pour the chicken stock into a large
saucepan and add the spring onions,
leek, five spice powder, ginger and
soy sauce. Cover and cook gently for
10 minutes.
2 Add the egg noodles to the
saucepan and cook gently for 5

minutes. Now add the sweetcorn
and chicken, and cook for 2 minutes
more.
3 Mix in the blended cornflour and
cook for about 1 minute, stirring,
until the soup is thickened and
smooth. Season to taste with salt
and pepper.
4 Ladle the soup into four warmed
bowls and serve at once.

Top tip Chinese five spice powder is
readily available in the spice rack at
your local supermarket.

Variation Substitute long grain rice for
the noodles, adding it with the soy
sauce in step 1 so that it has time to
cook. The Points will remain the same.

MINESTRONE

3 Points per recipe

Ⓥ Ⓥⓖ Serves 6

Preparation time: 15 minutes

Cooking time: 25 minutes

Calories per serving: 115

Freezing: recommended

Minestrone comes in many different guises, depending on the particular region of Italy. Literally meaning 'big soup', it's a winner when served as a satisfying starter or light meal.

low fat cooking spray

1 large onion, chopped

1 large carrot, chopped

150 g (5¹/₂ oz) swede or turnip, chopped

125 g (4¹/₂ oz) green beans, sliced

1 courgette, chopped

2 vegetable stock cubes, dissolved in 850 ml (1¹/₂ pints) boiling water

2 × 400 g cans of chopped tomatoes

2 teaspoons mixed dried Italian herbs

40 g (1¹/₂ oz) tiny pasta shapes

100 g (3¹/₂ oz) canned cannellini beans, drained and rinsed

2 tomatoes, skinned and chopped

salt and freshly ground black pepper

chopped fresh parsley, to garnish

1 Heat a large saucepan and spray it with low fat cooking spray. Add the onion, carrot, swede or turnip, green beans and courgette, and sauté them gently for about 3 minutes.

2 Pour in the vegetable stock and canned tomatoes, and add the dried herbs. Bring to the boil, and then reduce the heat. Cover and simmer very gently for about 15 minutes.

3 Add the pasta and canned beans to the saucepan with the tomatoes. Cook for 10 minutes more, or until the pasta is tender. Check the seasoning, adding salt and pepper to taste.

4 Serve the soup in six warmed bowls, garnished with parsley.

Top tip Cool, cover and refrigerate any leftover soup, and use it within two days, or you can freeze the soup for up to two months.

Variation For a No Point soup with an Italian flavour, omit the pasta and canned beans.

Minestrone: Sample the flavours of Italy for only ¹/₂ a Point.

TORTILLA CHIPS AND DIPS

15¹/₂ Points per recipe

Ⓥ Serves 4

Preparation and cooking time: 20 minutes

Calories per serving: 220

Freezing: not recommended

These Mexican style tortilla chips make very tasty nibbles when you have guests. Points are kept to a minimum because they're baked, rather than deep fried.

4 spicy tomato or plain soft flour tortillas

low fat cooking spray

For the sour cream style dip

150 ml (5 fl oz) half fat crème fraîche

1 tablespoon chopped fresh chives

freshly ground black pepper

For the chilli dip

1 small red onion, chopped very finely

¹/₄ cucumber, chopped very finely

1 medium fresh green chilli, de-seeded and chopped finely

juice of 1 lime or ¹/₂ lemon

¹/₂ teaspoon sugar

salt and freshly ground black pepper

1 Preheat the oven to Gas Mark 6/ 200°C /fan oven 180°C.

2 Stack the tortillas into a pile and cut them into quarters. Cut each quarter into three or four pieces. Spread out the pieces on baking sheets and spray them with low fat

cooking spray – do this in batches if you need to.

3 Bake for 8–10 minutes, until the tortilla chips are crisp and golden.

4 Meanwhile, make the dips. For the sour cream style dip, combine the crème fraîche and chives. Season with a little black pepper. For the chilli dip, mix together the onion, cucumber, chilli, lime or lemon juice, sugar and seasoning. Transfer the dips to separate serving bowls.

5 Cool the tortilla chips, and then serve with the dips.

Top tip Flavour plain soft tortillas with a little chilli powder and mixed dried herbs. Lightly spray the tortillas with low fat cooking spray and then sprinkle on the No Point flavourings.

FRENCH ONION SOUP

12 Points per recipe

Serves 4

Preparation time: 20 minutes

Cooking time: 30 minutes

Calories per serving: 190

Freezing: recommended (before adding French bread and cheese)

The secret for a great flavour is to brown the onions well before adding the stock.

4 teaspoons polyunsaturated margarine

2 large onions, sliced into rings

25 g (1 oz) plain white flour

2 beef stock cubes, dissolved in 850 ml (1½ pints) boiling water

1 bay leaf

4 × 15 g (½ oz) slices of French bread

50 g (1¾ oz) Gruyère cheese, grated

salt and freshly ground black pepper

1 Melt the margarine in a large saucepan and add the onions. Cook them gently over a medium heat until they are very brown – almost caramelised. This is important to give the soup its authentic flavour.

2 Stir the flour into the onions and then gradually add the beef stock, stirring constantly. Bring to the boil and add the bay leaf. Cover, reduce the heat and cook gently for 30 minutes, until the onions are tender.

3 Preheat the grill. Remove and discard the bay leaf. Season the soup with salt and pepper, and ladle it into four heatproof bowls.

4 Float a slice of French bread on the top of each bowlful and sprinkle with the grated cheese. Place the bowls under the grill and heat until the cheese bubbles and browns.

HOUMOUS WITH PITTA

15½ Points per recipe

Ⓥ Ⓥg *Serves 6*

Preparation time: 10 minutes

Calories per serving: 130

Freezing: not recommended

This has all the flavour of shop bought varieties but just a fraction of the Points.

400 g can of chick peas

1 large garlic clove, chopped roughly

2 teaspoons toasted sesame oil or olive oil

2 tablespoons lemon juice

salt and freshly ground black pepper

To serve

chopped fresh coriander or parsley

6 mini pitta breads

1 Drain the chick peas, reserving 2 tablespoons of their liquid. Tip them into a blender or food processor with the reserved liquid. Alternatively, mash the chick peas with a potato masher. Add the garlic, sesame or olive oil and lemon juice, and then blend for about 20 seconds until the mixture is smooth.

2 Transfer the mixture to a serving bowl, adding salt and pepper, according to taste. You may wish to add a little more lemon juice too. Sprinkle with the chopped coriander or parsley.

3 Warm the pitta breads under the grill or in a toaster. Serve with the houmous.

Variation If you want to reduce the Points to 1½ per portion, serve the houmous with No Point vegetable crudités instead of the pitta bread.

GARLIC PRAWNS

5 Points per recipe

Serves 2

Preparation and cooking time: 10 minutes + 15 minutes marinating

Calories per serving: 215

Freezing: not recommended

One bite of these divine garlic prawns and your tastebuds will be transported to Spain, where they are served as a mouthwatering starter.

1 garlic clove, crushed

finely grated zest and juice of ½ lemon

225 g (8 oz) cooked tiger prawns, with tails

1 teaspoon olive oil

1 tablespoon chopped fresh parsley

Maldon salt, or ordinary salt and freshly ground black pepper

2 × 25 g (1 oz) slices of French bread, to serve

1 Mix the garlic with the lemon zest and lemon juice in a shallow dish. Add the prawns and season them with black pepper. Cover and leave to marinate for 15 minutes.

2 Heat a heavy based frying pan, and add the prawns and their marinade. Cook over a high heat for 2–3 minutes, turning the prawns regularly.

3 Divide the prawns between two warm serving plates, drizzling any remaining juices over them. Sprinkle each portion with half a teaspoon of olive oil and a little parsley. Season with Maldon or ordinary salt according to taste and serve with the bread to mop up the juices.

Variation Replace the lemon half with 1 lime for a slightly sharper taste. Add a few drops of Tabasco sauce for a spicy flavour. The Points will remain the same.

VEGETABLE SAMOSAS

$\frac{1}{2}$ POINT

7 Points per recipe

Ⓥ Makes 20

Preparation time: 30 minutes

Cooking time: 30 minutes

Calories per samosa: 35

Freezing: recommended

Samosas are a tasty nibble – ideal for starters, snacks and buffets. Those served in Indian restaurants or bought from supermarkets are deep fried and very high in Points. You'll be far better off making your own, as these are baked to keep the Points to a minimum.

275 g (9½ oz) potatoes, peeled and cut into 1 cm (½ inch) cubes

1 small carrot, chopped finely

low fat cooking spray

1 small onion, chopped finely

1 garlic clove, crushed

50 g (1¾ oz) frozen peas, defrosted

1 teaspoon medium curry powder

1 tablespoon chopped fresh coriander

5 sheets of filo pastry (approximately 30 cm × 40 cm/12 inches × 16 inches), defrosted if frozen

salt and freshly ground black pepper

To serve

4 tomatoes, chopped finely

1 small red onion, chopped finely

2 tablespoons chopped fresh mint

1 In a large saucepan, cook the potatoes and carrot in lightly salted, boiling water for about 10 minutes, until tender. Drain well and then partially mash them with a fork.

2 Spray a non stick frying pan with low fat cooking spray. Add the onion and garlic, and cook until lightly browned.

3 Mix the onion, garlic, peas, curry powder and coriander into the mashed potato and carrot mixture. Season with salt and pepper. Allow to cool.

4 Preheat the oven to Gas Mark 4/ 180°C/fan oven 160°C. Spray two baking sheets with low fat cooking spray.

5 Cut the stack of filo pastry sheets into strips measuring approximately 30 cm × 10 cm (12 inches × 4 inches).

6 Place a tablespoon of the samosa mixture at one end of a strip of pastry. Fold the corners over and over to make a pastry triangle, enclosing all the filling. Repeat the process to make 20 samosas. Lay them on the baking sheets as you prepare them.

7 Lightly spray the samosas with low fat cooking spray and then bake them for 25–30 minutes, until golden.

8 Meanwhile, mix together the tomatoes, onion and mint. Serve this with the samosas.

Top tip Filo pastry soon dries out, so it's important to keep it covered as you work – use a clean, damp tea towel or clingfilm.

Variation Use mint in the samosas instead of coriander, if you prefer.

Vegetable Samosas: Only ½ a Point each.

meals
for one or two

At Weight Watchers, we realise that for people with busy lifestyles, it is often going to be impractical to sit down to eat with the whole family, and so it is likely that sometimes you will be cooking for yourself or just for two. At times like this, it can be all too easy to pick up food that is quick and convenient, without giving much thought to the Points. This chapter is here to provide you with inspiration for times like this, and to show you that there is a world of easy, tasty, low Point meals just waiting to be explored.

JAMBALAYA

5½ Points per recipe
Serves 1
Preparation time and cooking time:
30 minutes
Calories per serving: 400
Freezing: not recommended

This easy and delicious Cajun dish from the deep south in the USA was influenced by the flavours of Spain.

50 g (1¾ oz) long grain rice

low fat cooking spray

1 celery stick, sliced

3 spring onions, chopped

½ small green pepper, de-seeded and chopped

1 small garlic clove, crushed

½ teaspoon Cajun seasoning, or according to taste

½ teaspoon fresh thyme leaves or ¼ teaspoon dried thyme

15 g (½ oz) chorizo sausage, sliced

1 tomato, chopped

50 g (1¾ oz) skinless, boneless cooked chicken, chopped

50 g (1¾ oz) large peeled prawns, defrosted if frozen

salt and freshly ground black pepper

sprigs of fresh thyme, to garnish

1 Cook the rice in plenty of boiling, lightly salted water for about 12 minutes until tender.

2 Meanwhile, heat a large frying pan or wok and lightly spray it with low fat cooking spray. Add the celery, spring onions, green pepper and garlic. Sauté them for about 3 minutes, until softened.

3 Add the Cajun seasoning, thyme, chorizo sausage, tomato and chicken. Cook gently, stirring occasionally, for a further 5 minutes.

4 Drain the rice thoroughly and then add it to the frying pan, stirring well to combine everything. Add the prawns and cook for another 2–3 minutes, until they are heated through. Season with salt and pepper and then serve, garnished with sprigs of thyme.

Top tip If you can't find Cajun seasoning, use 1 teaspoon of mild chilli powder and a pinch of cayenne pepper, adding more or less according to taste.

Variation Omit the sausage and chicken for a meatless version, and add another 50 g (1¾ oz) of prawns. The Points per serving will be 4.

Jambalaya:
A delicious, spicy
Cajun dish for
only 5½ Points.

Ham and Mushroom Pizza: Enjoy half a Ham and Mushroom Pizza for only 5½ Points.

HAM AND MUSHROOM PIZZA

10½ Points per recipe
Serves 2
Preparation time: 10 minutes
Cooking time: 15 minutes
Calories per serving: 325
Freezing: recommended

Thank goodness the Italians invented pizza – we love it! Keep a few thin and crispy pizza bases in your freezer; they're so handy for creating a quick and tasty meal.

30 cm (12 inch) thin and crispy pizza base
2 tablespoons tomato purée
low fat cooking spray
1 small onion, chopped
6 closed cup mushrooms, sliced
50 g (1¾ oz) wafer thin ham, torn into pieces
1 teaspoon Italian mixed dried herbs
salt and freshly ground black pepper
50 g (1¾ oz) half fat Cheddar cheese, grated

1 Preheat the oven to Gas Mark 6/ 200°C/fan oven 180°C and heat a large baking sheet.
2 Spread the pizza base with the tomato purée.
3 Heat a non stick frying pan, and then lightly spray it with low fat cooking spray. Add the onion and mushrooms, and cook gently for about 6–8 minutes, until softened. Cool slightly, and then scatter them evenly over the pizza base.
4 Distribute the wafer thin ham over the pizza, and then sprinkle over the herbs. Season, then scatter the cheese evenly over the top.
5 Transfer the pizza to the hot baking sheet and cook for 12–15 minutes, until the cheese bubbles and browns.

STEAK AU POIVRE

6 Points per recipe
Serves 1
Preparation and cooking time: 15 minutes
Calories per serving: 235
Freezing: not recommended

Treat yourself to a juicy fillet steak with lots of No Point vegetables for a filling and delicious meal.

1 rounded teaspoon black or green peppercorns
100 g (3½ oz) fillet steak, trimmed
low fat cooking spray
1 tablespoon brandy
2 tablespoons half fat crème fraîche
Maldon salt or sea salt

To serve
No Point vegetables, such as courgettes, mange tout peas and cauliflower
chopped fresh parsley, (optional)

1 Crush the peppercorns coarsely, either by using a mortar and pestle or a rolling pin.
2 Press both sides of the fillet steak firmly on to the crushed peppercorns.
3 Heat a heavy based frying pan and lightly spray it with low fat cooking spray. Over a high heat, add the steak and allow it to sear and brown for about 30 seconds. Turn it over and sear it on the other side. Reduce the heat to medium hot, and cook the steak for another 2–5 minutes on each side, or until cooked to your liking. Transfer to a warm serving plate, season with salt and keep warm.
4 Add the brandy to the pan and let it bubble up for a few moments. Spoon in the crème fraîche, heat for about 30 seconds, and then pour this sauce over the steak.

5 Serve with some No Point vegetables and garnish with the chopped fresh parsley, if desired.

Top tips Use sirloin or rump steak instead of fillet if you prefer the flavour. The Points per serving will be 6 and 5½ respectively.

A small helping of low fat oven baked chips will add a further 2 Points to your meal.

Steak au Poivre: Enjoy steak with chips for 8 Points.

Teriyaki Noodles: Oodles of noodles for only 4 Points.

TERIYAKI NOODLES

4 POINTS

8¹/₂ Points per recipe

Ⓥ Ⓥᵉ Serves 2

Preparation and cooking time:
20 minutes + 1 hour marinating
Calories per serving: 370
Freezing: not recommended

Rice noodles are sold dried and need to be soaked before use – just follow the pack directions, and then use them in this delicious stir fry.

2 tablespoons teriyaki sauce or dark soy sauce
1 tablespoon lime or lemon juice
1–2 teaspoons chilli sauce, according to taste
1 tablespoon chopped fresh coriander
225 g (8 oz) firm tofu, cubed
100 g (3¹/₂ oz) rice noodles
1 teaspoon stir fry oil or sesame oil
1 garlic clove, crushed
250 g (9 oz) No Point fresh or frozen stir fry vegetables
60 g (2 oz) fresh beansprouts
salt and freshly ground black pepper
a handful of spring onions, shredded into fine strips, to garnish

1 Mix together the Teriyaki sauce or soy sauce, lime or lemon juice, chilli sauce and chopped coriander in a non metallic bowl. Add the tofu cubes, stir well, cover and refrigerate for at least 1 hour.

2 When ready to cook, put the noodles into a large bowl and cover them with warm water. Leave them to soak for about 5 minutes, or follow the pack instructions, then drain well.

3 Heat the stir fry oil or sesame oil in a wok or large frying pan. Add the garlic and vegetables (but not the beansprouts) and stir fry them over a high heat for 2–3 minutes.

4 Add the noodles to the wok or frying pan and cook, stirring, for another 2 minutes. Now add the beansprouts and tofu with its marinade.

5 Cook over a medium to high heat, stirring gently, for 1–2 minutes until all the ingredients are heated through. Check the seasoning, adding salt and pepper to taste and then serve, garnished with the spring onions.

Variation Use peeled prawns instead of tofu, if you prefer. The Points per serving will be 4¹/₂.

AMERICAN BEEFBURGER

6 POINTS

6 Points per recipe

Serves 1

Preparation and cooking time:
25 minutes
Calories per serving: 335
Freezing: recommended

Juicy and full of flavour, this burger is made with prime extra lean beef to keep the Points as low as possible.

110 g (4 oz) extra lean minced beef
¹/₄ small red onion, chopped very finely
1 small garlic clove, crushed
¹/₄ teaspoon dried thyme
¹/₂ teaspoon dried oregano
a few drops of Tabasco sauce
1 small egg white, beaten lightly
salt and freshly ground black pepper

To serve

50 g (1³/₄ oz) burger bun
shredded lettuce
1 tomato slice
1 dill pickle (large gherkin), sliced

1 Preheat the grill. In a large bowl, mix all the burger ingredients together until thoroughly combined.

2 Using your hands, shape the mixture into a large burger.

3 Place the burger on the grill rack and cook for about 6–7 minutes on each side, until well browned.

4 To serve, place the burger in the bun and top with plenty of shredded lettuce, the tomato slice and the dill pickle.

Variations You could make this burger with lean lamb or turkey mince. The Points per serving would be 7 and 4¹/₂ respectively.

THAI VEGETABLE CURRY

5½ Points per recipe

Serves 2
Preparation time: 15 minutes
Cooking time: 35 minutes
Calories per serving: 190
Freezing: recommended

The flavours of Thailand – lemongrass, coriander, shallots and curry paste – combine together in this warming vegetable curry to give you a filling, healthy and delicious meal.

low fat cooking spray
4 shallots or 1 small onion, sliced
1 garlic clove, crushed
½ small butternut squash, peeled, de-seeded and cut into chunks
1 courgette, sliced
1 red pepper, de-seeded and sliced thickly

50 g (1¾ oz) fine green beans, halved
1 vegetable stock cube, dissolved in 300 ml (10 fl oz) boiling water
150 ml (5 fl oz) 88 % fat free coconut milk
½ teaspoon ready prepared 'fresh' lemongrass
½ teaspoon ready prepared 'fresh' root ginger
1–2 teaspoons Thai red or green curry paste, according to taste
1 tablespoon chopped fresh coriander
salt and freshly ground black pepper
coriander sprigs, to garnish

1 Lightly spray a wok or large frying pan with low fat cooking spray. Add the shallots or onion and garlic and sauté them for 2–3 minutes, until softened.

2 Add the butternut squash, courgette, pepper, beans, vegetable stock, coconut milk, lemongrass, ginger and curry paste. Simmer for 25–30 minutes, until the vegetables are tender and the liquid has reduced by about one third.

3 Add the coriander and season to taste. Serve the curry garnished with coriander sprigs.

Thai Vegetable Curry: Exquisite Thai flavours for just 3 Points.

TAGLIATELLE CARBONARA

13 Points per recipe

Ⓥ *if following variation*
Serves 2
Preparation time: 10 minutes
Cooking time: 15 minutes
Calories per serving: 375
Freezing: not recommended

This classic Italian recipe is so easy to make for two.

110 g (4 oz) tagliatelle or linguine
low fat cooking spray
1 rasher of lean back bacon, snipped into pieces
4 spring onions, chopped finely
1 garlic clove, peeled and left whole
100 g tub of low fat soft cheese with herbs

1 small egg
100 ml (3½ fl oz) skimmed milk
15 g (½ oz) finely grated Parmesan cheese
1 tablespoon chopped fresh parsley
salt and freshly ground black pepper
sprigs of fresh parsley, to garnish

1 Cook the tagliatelle or linguine in a large pan of lightly salted, boiling water for about 8 minutes, or until just tender.

2 Meanwhile, heat a frying pan and spray it with low fat cooking spray. Add the bacon and spring onions, and sauté them with the garlic clove for about 5 minutes, until the onions are softened. Remove the garlic clove and discard – it has just been used to impart a little flavour to the finished dish.

3 Beat the soft cheese and egg together in a mixing bowl, and then add the bacon and spring onions, stirring until the mixture is combined. Add the milk, half the Parmesan cheese and the parsley. Season with a little salt and pepper.

4 Drain the pasta, reserving two tablespoons of the cooking liquid, and then return it to the saucepan with the reserved liquid. Stir in the egg and cheese mixture, and heat gently for 2–3 minutes, stirring, until it has cooked and thickened slightly.

5 Serve the pasta, sprinkled with the remaining Parmesan cheese and garnished with sprigs of parsley.

Variation For a vegetarian alternative, omit the bacon and add 50 g (1¾ oz) of sliced button mushrooms. The Points per serving will be 5½.

SPANISH MEATBALLS

12½ Points per recipe

Serves 2

Preparation time: 15 minutes

Cooking time: 25 minutes

Calories per serving: 420

Freezing: recommended

These little lamb meatballs are dry fried, then cooked in a tasty tomato sauce for an easy to make meal with a Spanish flavour.

150 g (5½ oz) lean minced lamb

1 small onion, chopped finely

1 garlic clove, crushed

2 teaspoons mixed dried herbs

1 small egg white, beaten lightly

2 tablespoons brandy

100 g (3½ oz) button mushrooms, sliced

300 ml (10 fl oz) passata

1 tablespoon tomato purée

1 teaspoon paprika

1 vegetable stock cube, dissolved in 150 ml (5 fl oz) boiling water

100 g (3½ oz) spaghetti or other pasta shapes

salt and freshly ground black pepper

chopped fresh parsley, to garnish

1 In a mixing bowl, combine the minced lamb, onion, garlic, dried herbs and egg white. Season with salt and pepper.

2 Using clean hands, form the mixture into small meatballs.

3 Heat a large non stick frying pan and add the meatballs, dry frying them until they are lightly browned. Pour in the brandy and let it bubble up for a few moments, and then add the mushrooms, passata, tomato purée, paprika and stock. Heat until simmering, and then cook gently for 20–25 minutes to reduce the liquid by about one third, stirring occasionally.

4 10 minutes before the end of the cooking time, cook the pasta in plenty of boiling, lightly salted water according to the packet instructions until just tender. Drain thoroughly.

5 Divide the pasta between two warmed plates and top with the meatballs and sauce. Garnish with plenty of chopped fresh parsley.

Top tip If you can't find passata, use a 400 g can of chopped tomatoes instead.

Variation Try using 100 g (3½ oz) rice instead of pasta. The Points will then be 6½ per serving.

SPAGHETTI BOLOGNESE

12½ Points per recipe

Ⓥ Ⓥ₉ *if following variation*

Serves 2

Preparation time: 25 minutes

Cooking time: 30 minutes

Calories per serving: 460

Freezing: recommended for the sauce only

This classic recipe for spaghetti bolognese proves that familiar dishes are just as tasty and enjoyable as ever.

low fat cooking spray

200 g (7 oz) extra lean minced beef

1 garlic clove, crushed

1 small onion, chopped

1 celery stick, chopped finely

400 g can of chopped tomatoes

1 tablespoon tomato purée

75 g (2¾ oz) mushrooms, sliced

1 beef stock cube

50 ml (2 fl oz) red wine

2 teaspoons Italian mixed dried herbs

100 g (3½ oz) spaghetti

salt and freshly ground black pepper

fresh herb sprigs, to garnish

1 Spray a large, heavy based saucepan or flameproof casserole dish with low fat cooking spray.

2 Add the mince, a small handful at a time, allowing it to seal and brown before adding the next handful.

3 Add the garlic, onion and celery and cook for about 5 minutes, stirring occasionally. Pour in the canned tomatoes and add the tomato purée and mushrooms. Heat and stir, and then crumble in the stock cube followed by the wine and dried herbs. Bring it all to the boil, and then reduce the heat and simmer gently for about 30 minutes, stirring from time to time. Season to taste.

4 About 15 minutes before you want to serve, cook the spaghetti in lightly salted, boiling water for about 8–10 minutes, according to pack instructions. Drain.

5 Divide the cooked spaghetti between two serving plates and spoon the bolognese sauce on top. Garnish with a few fresh sprigs of herbs and then serve.

Top tip Double up the quantities of bolognese mixture and freeze a batch for next time – remember to cool it as quickly as possible. Freeze for up to two months.

Variation For a vegetarian alternative, use 250 g (9 oz) Quorn mince instead of the beef and make sure you use a vegetable stock cube. The Points will be 4½ per serving.

STIR FRIED CHICKEN

4 Points per recipe

Serves 1

*Preparation and cooking time:
15 minutes*

Calories per serving: 350

Freezing: not recommended

This is a delightful Chinese dish that is wonderfully tasty, yet so easy to prepare.

30 g (1¼ oz) Chinese thread egg noodles

1 teaspoon sesame or vegetable oil

250 g (9 oz) prepared stir fry No Point vegetables (e.g. spring onions, pepper, carrot, broccoli, mange tout peas, mushrooms)

75 g (2¾ oz) skinless, roast chicken breast, sliced into strips

¼ teaspoon ready prepared 'fresh' root ginger

¼ teaspoon ready prepared 'fresh' garlic

1 teaspoon ready prepared 'fresh' coriander or parsley

¼ teaspoon Chinese five spice powder

1 tablespoon light soy sauce

salt and freshly ground black pepper

chopped fresh coriander or parsley, to garnish

1 Soak the noodles in boiling water for 6 minutes, or according to the pack instructions.

2 Meanwhile, heat the oil in a non stick wok or large frying pan. Add all the vegetables and the chicken. Stir fry over a high heat for 4–5 minutes. The vegetables should remain crisp, crunchy and colourful.

3 Drain the noodles thoroughly. Add them to the wok with the ginger, garlic, coriander or parsley, five spice powder and soy sauce. Stir fry for 1–2 minutes more to heat everything thoroughly.

4 Season the stir fry with salt and pepper. Serve on a warmed plate, garnished with fresh coriander or parsley.

Top tip You can buy small jars of ready prepared fresh ingredients such as ginger, garlic and herbs – so handy for small quantities. Once opened, they can be stored in the fridge for up to six weeks.

Variation Use your choice of stir fry vegetables – just make sure that they all have No Points.

Stir Fried Chicken: Simply delicious and only 4 Points.

**Lamb Rogan Josh:
Delicious with
basmati rice for
an incredible
6 Points.**

meat & poultry

In this chapter, you'll find some of the tastiest dishes from around the world. There are some that are probably very familiar to you, like Sweet and Sour Pork, Lasagne and Chicken Tikka Masala. Traditionally, these dishes tend to be high in Points, so here you'll find the healthier, low Point versions of some of your favourite meals...and they're just as delicious!

LAMB ROGAN JOSH

11½ Points per recipe

Serves 4

Preparation time: 20 minutes

Cooking time: 1 hour

Calories per serving: 315

Freezing: recommended

Rogan Josh is a rich, aromatic Indian curry with a distinctive red colour. Serve this accompanied by 4 tablespoons of cooked rice, adding an extra 3 Points.

low fat cooking spray
2 onions, sliced
500 g (1 lb 2 oz) lean lamb leg steak, cubed
1 garlic clove, crushed
1 teaspoon grated fresh root ginger or ready prepared 'fresh' ginger
1½ tablespoons rogan josh curry powder
400 g can of chopped tomatoes
2 carrots, sliced
1 lamb or chicken stock cube, dissolved in 150 ml (5 fl oz) boiling water
2 tablespoons tomato purée
1 tablespoon chopped fresh coriander
salt and freshly ground black pepper
fresh coriander sprigs, to garnish

1 Heat a large saucepan, and spray it with low fat cooking spray. Add the onions and cook, stirring, for 3–4 minutes until they are lightly browned.

2 Add the lamb, a handful at a time, and cook over a medium high heat until it is all sealed and browned. Add the garlic, ginger and rogan josh curry powder and cook, stirring, for 1 minute.

3 Add the canned tomatoes, carrots, stock, tomato purée and chopped coriander to the pan. Season with a little salt and black pepper and bring to the boil. Reduce the heat to low, then cover and simmer for about 1 hour, or until the lamb is very tender.

4 Check the seasoning, adding a little more salt and pepper, if necessary. Serve garnished with fresh coriander sprigs.

Top tips Why not make a refreshing No Point Indian salad, known as kachumba, to accompany the Rogan Josh? Roughly chop a couple of tomatoes, half a red onion and a 10 cm (4 inch) piece of cucumber. Mix in a de-seeded and finely chopped large fresh green chilli and a couple of tablespoons of chopped fresh coriander. Add a squeeze of lime or lemon juice, and season with salt and pepper.

Sharwoods and Sainsburys both make rogan josh curry powder.

HUNGARIAN GOULASH

13 Points per recipe
Serves 4
Preparation time: 20 minutes
Cooking time: 1½ hours
Calories per serving: 220
Freezing: recommended

Goulash is a rich, warming stew that originates from Hungary. It tastes all the better for its long, slow cooking.

low fat cooking spray
400 g (14 oz) lean stewing steak, cubed
1 large onion, sliced
1 garlic clove, crushed
1½ tablespoons paprika
400 g can of chopped tomatoes
1 tablespoon tomato purée
1 large green or red pepper, de-seeded and chopped
1 beef stock cube, dissolved in 425 ml (15 fl oz) hot water
1 tablespoon cornflour, blended with 3–4 tablespoons water
salt and freshly ground black pepper

To serve
4 tablespoons low fat plain yogurt
a handful of chopped fresh parsley

1 Spray a large non stick saucepan with low fat cooking spray. Heat the pan and then add the meat a handful at a time, making sure that each handful has sealed and browned before adding the next.

2 Add the onion and garlic and sauté for about 3 minutes, until softened. Stir in the paprika.

3 Add the tomatoes, tomato purée, green or red pepper and stock. Bring to the boil, reduce the heat, then cover and simmer for 1½ hours, or until the meat is very tender. Check the level of liquid from time to time, topping up with a little extra water if necessary.

4 Season the goulash with salt and pepper. Add the blended cornflour and stir until the sauce is thickened. Cook for 1–2 minutes.

5 Spoon the goulash on to warmed plates, topping each portion with 1 tablespoon of yogurt. Serve, sprinkled with parsley.

Top tip This goulash tastes delicious with 100 g (3½ oz) plain boiled potatoes. Add an extra 1 Point per serving.

BEEF BOURGUIGNON

18 Points per recipe
Serves 4
Preparation time: 20 minutes
Cooking time: 2–2½ hours
Calories per serving: 295
Freezing: recommended

This classic French beef casserole is made with red wine and a splash of brandy to give a fantastic flavour – c'est magnifique!

low fat cooking spray
500 g (1 lb 2 oz) lean braising steak, cut into chunks
1 rasher of lean back bacon, snipped into pieces
8 shallots or small onions, peeled and left whole
2 garlic cloves, chopped
1 celery stick, chopped
2 tablespoons brandy
150 ml (5 fl oz) Burgundy or other red wine
1 beef stock cube, dissolved in 150 ml (5 fl oz) boiling water
1 bay leaf
1 tablespoon cornflour, blended with 3 tablespoons cold water
salt and freshly ground black pepper

1 Preheat the oven to Gas Mark 3/ 160°C/fan oven 140°C.

2 Heat a large flameproof casserole dish on the hob and spray it with low fat cooking spray. Add the beef, a handful at a time, and cook over a high heat until it is sealed and browned all over.

3 Add the bacon, shallots or onions, garlic and celery. Cook, stirring, for 2–3 minutes. Pour in the brandy and allow it to bubble up, and then add the wine and stock. Add the bay leaf and season with a little salt and pepper. Cover, transfer to the oven and cook for 2–2½ hours.

4 Lift the casserole from the oven and place it over a very low heat on the hob. Remove the bay leaf.

5 Add the cornflour mixture and stir well. Cook for 1–2 minutes until the sauce is thickened. Check the seasoning, adding more salt and pepper if needed, and then serve on four warmed plates.

Top tip Mashed potatoes are the perfect accompaniment to this delicious casserole – but remember to add the extra Points. A 60 g (2 oz) scoop, made without fat, adds ½ a Point per serving.

CHICKEN TIKKA MASALA

4 POINTS

17 Points per recipe

ⓥ *if following variation*

Serves 4

Preparation time: 15 minutes + 1 hour marinating

Cooking time: 25 minutes

Calories per serving: 280

Freezing: recommended

This colourful, creamy dish is one of the nation's favourites. Try this fantastic low Point version.

2 tablespoons tikka masala curry paste

150 g tub of 0% fat Greek style yogurt

450 g (1 lb) skinless, boneless chicken breasts, cut into chunks

1 teaspoon vegetable oil

1 red onion, sliced thinly

1 teaspoon grated fresh root ginger or 1 teaspoon ready prepared 'fresh' ginger

400 g can of chopped tomatoes

150 ml (5 fl oz) chicken stock

2 tablespoons chopped fresh coriander

100 g (3¹/₂ oz) basmati rice

salt and freshly ground black pepper

5 cm (2 inch) piece of cucumber, chopped finely

sprigs of fresh coriander, to garnish

1 Put the curry paste into a non metallic bowl and mix in the yogurt, reserving 60 g (2 oz) of it for later. Add the chicken, stir well and then cover and leave to marinate in the fridge for at least 1 hour or overnight.

2 When ready to cook, heat the vegetable oil in a large saucepan and add most of the onion, reserving some for garnish. Sauté for 1–2 minutes and then add the ginger and marinated chicken mixture. Cook for 2–3 minutes.

3 Add the tomatoes, stock and chopped coriander to the saucepan. Bring up to the boil, then reduce the heat and simmer, uncovered, over a low heat for 20–25 minutes. Season to taste with salt and pepper, if needed.

4 When the chicken has simmered for 10 minutes, put the rice on to cook in plenty of lightly salted, boiling water – it will take about 12 minutes.

5 Serve the rice with the cooked chicken, garnished with the reserved yogurt, remaining red onion, cucumber and coriander sprigs.

Variation Use Quorn chunks instead of chicken for a vegetarian alternative. The Points per serving will remain the same.

Chicken Tikka Masala: A wonderful, creamy curry for only 4 Points with rice.

Moroccan Lamb Tagine: A delicious North African stew, served with couscous for 4½ Points.

MOROCCAN LAMB TAGINE

18 Points per recipe

Serves 4

Preparation time: 20 minutes

Cooking time: 1 hour 40 minutes

Calories per serving: 370

Freezing: recommended

This fragrant Moroccan lamb stew is slow cooked with aromatic spices to give a delicious, mellow flavour.

---

low fat cooking spray

450 g (1 lb) lean lamb leg steak, cubed

1 large onion, chopped

1 teaspoon ground cinnamon

1 teaspoon ground coriander

1 teaspoon ground ginger

1 lamb stock cube, dissolved in 600 ml (20 fl oz) boiling water

100 g (3½ oz) ready to eat dried apricots

100 g (3½ oz) couscous

salt and freshly ground black pepper

fresh coriander sprigs, to garnish

---

1 Heat a large, heavy based saucepan and spray it with low fat cooking spray. Add the lamb, a handful at a time, until it is browned on all sides.

2 Add the onion and cook for 2–3 minutes, and then add the cinnamon, ground coriander and ginger. Cook for another 2 minutes.

3 Pour in the stock and bring to the boil. Reduce the heat, cover and simmer for about 1¼ hours until the meat is very tender.

4 Add the apricots to the stew and cook, uncovered, for another 15–20 minutes, so that the liquid reduces.

5 Meanwhile, prepare the couscous according to the pack instructions.

6 Season the lamb with salt and pepper and serve it with the couscous, garnished with fresh coriander sprigs.

LASAGNE

25½ Points per recipe

v *if following variation*

Serves 4

Preparation time: 30 minutes

Cooking time: 45–50 minutes

Calories per serving: 395

Freezing: recommended

Lasagne is one of the all time favourite Italian dishes. Try this delicious version, it has far fewer Points than the equivalent ready meal.

---

300 g (10½ oz) extra lean minced beef

1 onion, chopped

175 g (6 oz) mushrooms, sliced

400 g can of chopped tomatoes with garlic

1 beef stock cube, dissolved in 150 ml (5 fl oz) boiling water

2 teaspoons mixed dried Italian herbs

300 ml (10 fl oz) skimmed milk

3 tablespoons plain white flour

1 tablespoon polyunsaturated margarine

50 g (1¾ oz) half fat mature Cheddar cheese, grated

110 g (4 oz) no pre cook lasagne sheets

salt and freshly ground black pepper

---

1 Preheat the oven to Gas Mark 5/ 190°C/fan oven 170°C.

2 Heat a large saucepan and add the mince a handful at a time, dry frying it until sealed and browned. Add the onion and sauté for another 2–3 minutes, until the onion has softened.

3 Add the mushrooms, tomatoes, stock and herbs to the saucepan. Bring up to the boil, then reduce the heat and simmer for 15–20 minutes without a lid, until reduced slightly. Remove from the heat. Season to taste with salt and pepper.

4 To make the sauce, put the milk, flour and margarine into a medium non stick saucepan. Heat, stirring constantly with a small wire whisk, until the mixture is thickened and smooth. Remove from the heat and stir in most of the cheese. Season with salt and pepper.

5 Spoon half the beef mixture into an oblong ovenproof dish. Lay half the lasagne sheets on top. Spread 2–3 tablespoonfuls of the cheese sauce over these sheets and top with the remaining meat mixture. Lay the rest of the lasagne sheets on top, and then spread the rest of the sauce over the surface. Sprinkle with the reserved cheese.

6 Bake for 45–50 minutes until golden brown and bubbling.

Top tip It's vital to use a proper measuring spoon for the flour, and use level tablespoons, otherwise the sauce will be too thick.

Variation For a vegetarian lasagne, use a 350 g (12 oz) pack of Quorn mince, and make sure that you use a vegetable stock cube. The Points per serving will be 5.

Lasagne: Everyone's favourite for only 6½ Points.

COQ AU VIN

11 Points per recipe
Serves 4
Preparation time: 25 minutes
Cooking time: 30 minutes
Calories per serving: 210
Freezing: recommended

This classic French favourite tastes superb. It features chicken in a red wine sauce with mushrooms and shallots – making it a perfect meal anytime.

low fat cooking spray
8 shallots or small onions, halved
2 garlic cloves, crushed
4 × 140 g (5 oz) skinless, boneless chicken breasts
125 ml (4 fl oz) red wine

1 chicken stock cube, dissolved in 300 ml (10 fl oz) boiling water
175 g (6 oz) button mushrooms, halved
1 bay leaf
1 tablespoon cornflour, blended with 3 tablespoons cold water
salt and freshly ground black pepper

1 Heat a large frying pan or saucepan and spray it with low fat cooking spray. Add the shallots or onions and garlic, and sauté them for about 5 minutes, until they begin to turn brown. Push them to one side of the pan.

2 Add the chicken breasts to the pan and seal them quickly on both sides. Pour in the wine and let it bubble up for a few seconds. Add the chicken stock, mushrooms and bay leaf. Cover and simmer gently for about 30 minutes, until the chicken is tender.

3 Stir the blended cornflour into the pan. Heat, stirring constantly, until the sauce is thickened and smooth. Check the seasoning, adding salt and pepper. Remove the bay leaf and serve on four warmed plates.

Top tip Serve this dish with 100 g (3½ oz) new potatoes, accompanied by plenty of No Point vegetables, such as courgettes and broccoli adding 1 Point per serving.

MOUSSAKA

26½ Points per recipe
Ⓥ if following variation
Serves 4
Preparation time: 30 minutes
Cooking time: 45 minutes
Calories per serving: 360
Freezing: recommended

Moussaka is a baked Greek dish of minced lamb layered with aubergines and potatoes, topped with a creamy cheese sauce...delicious!

1 onion, chopped finely
2 garlic cloves, crushed
300 g (10½ oz) lean minced lamb
400 g can of chopped tomatoes with herbs
1 lamb or vegetable stock cube dissolved in 150 ml (5 fl oz) boiling water

2 tablespoons cornflour, blended with 5 tablespoons cold water
1 large aubergine, sliced
400 g (14 oz) potatoes, parboiled and sliced
1 egg
125 g tub of low fat soft cheese
150 ml (5 fl oz) 0% fat Greek style plain yogurt
25 g (1 oz) half fat mature Cheddar cheese, grated
salt and freshly ground black pepper

1 Preheat the oven to Gas Mark 5/ 190°C/fan oven 170°C.

2 Dry fry the onion, garlic and minced lamb in a large saucepan for about 5–6 minutes, until browned.

3 Add the tomatoes and stock, bring to the boil, then reduce the heat and simmer for 10 minutes without a lid. Add the blended cornflour and stir until thickened. Season with salt and pepper.

4 Spoon half the mince mixture into a large ovenproof baking dish. Lay the aubergine slices on top. Spread the remaining mince mixture over them, and then arrange the sliced potatoes on top in an overlapping layer.

5 Beat together the egg, soft cheese, yogurt and seasoning. Spread this over the potatoes. Sprinkle with the cheese and then bake for about 45 minutes, until the topping is set and golden brown.

Variation For a vegetarian version, substitute Quorn mince for the lamb and use a vegetable stock cube. The Points per serving will be 4½.

Coq au Vin: A taste of France for only 4 Points with potatoes.

Sweet and Sour Pork: Enjoy this classic Chinese dish for only 4½ Points.

SWEET AND SOUR PORK

4½ Points per recipe

Ⓥ Ⓥⓖ *if following variation*
Serves 1
Preparation time: 20 minutes
Cooking time: 20 minutes
Calories per serving: 380
Freezing: recommended

When you choose this popular dish at a Chinese restaurant or have it as a takeaway, you're likely to be using lots of Points. It's much better to enjoy this home made version, which has all the flavour but few of the Points.

1 teaspoon cornflour
1–2 teaspoons chilli sauce
1 teaspoon light or dark muscovado sugar
2 teaspoons rice or white wine vinegar
1 tablespoon light soy sauce
low fat cooking spray

100 g (3½ oz) lean pork shoulder, cut into strips
1 small garlic clove, crushed
1 small onion, sliced
1 small carrot, cut into fine strips
25 g (1 oz) mange tout peas, sliced
½ chicken or vegetable stock cube, dissolved in 100 ml (3½ fl oz) boiling water
1 tomato, skinned and quartered
salt and freshly ground black pepper

To serve

75 g (2¾ oz) hot, cooked long grain rice
coriander sprigs or finely chopped spring onions (optional)

1 In a small jug or bowl, mix together the cornflour, chilli sauce, sugar, vinegar and soy sauce.
2 Heat a wok or large frying pan and lightly spray it with low fat cooking spray. Add the pork, stir frying it over a high heat for 3–4 minutes to seal and brown it.
3 Add the garlic, onion, carrot and mange tout peas and stir fry for 2 minutes. Pour in the stock and bring to the boil. Reduce the heat and simmer gently for 15–20 minutes, or until the pork is tender.
4 Mix in the tomato. Then add the blended cornflour mixture, stirring as you do so. Cook for 2 minutes, until the sauce is thickened. Check the seasoning, adding salt and pepper, to taste.
5 Serve in a bowl with the hot, cooked rice, garnished with coriander sprigs or finely chopped spring onions, if using.

Variation For a vegetarian version, use 100 g (3½ oz) Quorn cubes instead of the pork, and marinate them in the cornflour mixture for 20–30 minutes before you start to cook. Add them after the tomatoes in step 4 and remember to use a vegetable stock cube. The Points per serving will be 3½.

JAMAICAN JERK CHICKEN

13 Points per recipe

Serves 2
Preparation time: 10 minutes
Cooking time: 25–30 minutes
Calories per serving: 475
Freezing: recommended

Enjoy the exotic flavours of the Caribbean in this easy recipe.

low fat cooking spray
1 tablespoon polenta or plain flour
½ tablespoon Jamaican jerk seasoning
2 × 165 g (5¾ oz) skinless chicken breasts
1 small egg white, beaten lightly with 2 teaspoons of water

75 g (2¾ oz) long grain rice
200 g (7 oz) canned red kidney beans, drained and rinsed
salt and freshly ground black pepper
chopped fresh parsley, to garnish
2 tomatoes, quartered, to serve

1 Preheat the oven to Gas Mark 6/ 200°C/fan oven 180°C. Spray a roasting pan with low fat cooking spray.
2 On a large plate, mix the polenta or flour with the jerk seasoning, salt and pepper.
3 Brush the chicken with the egg white and then toss it in the seasoning mixture to coat it on all sides. Place the chicken in the roasting pan and bake it in the oven for 25–30 minutes, until it is tender.
4 When the chicken has been in the oven for 15 minutes, put the rice on to cook in boiling, lightly salted water. Cook for about 12 minutes, or until tender – adding the red kidney beans for the final 3–4 minutes to heat them through.
5 Drain the rice and beans, and rinse them with boiling water. Divide the rice mixture between two warmed serving plates and place the chicken on top. Sprinkle with plenty of chopped fresh parsley and serve with the tomatoes.

Top tip Look out for Jamaican jerk seasoning in the spice racks or speciality food section of your local supermarket. It is quite fiery, so add a little at a time, according to your taste.

vegetarian
main courses

Recipes from Italy, Greece, Mexico, India, Thailand and China fill the following pages, giving you an insight into easy vegetarian dishes from around the world. Most of them are very quick and easy – and you'll love the results. So whether you're a full time vegetarian, or a meat eater that loves the occasional vegetarian meal, there are dishes here to suit all tastes.

SWEET AND SOUR STIR FRY

16 Points per recipe

(V) *Serves 4*

Preparation and cooking time:
25 minutes
Calories per serving: 300
Freezing: not recommended

Choose your favourite stir fry vegetables to make this quick and easy supper with its delicious sweet and sour sauce.

3 tablespoons soy sauce

1 tablespoon clear honey

1 tablespoon rice or white wine vinegar

1 teaspoon chilli sauce

1 teaspoon cornflour

100 g (3½ oz) thread egg noodles

low fat cooking spray

3 eggs

2 tablespoons skimmed milk

1 tablespoon stir fry oil or sesame oil

1 garlic clove, crushed

1 teaspoon finely grated fresh root ginger, or ready prepared 'fresh' ginger

450 g (1 lb) No Point stir fry vegetables, fresh or frozen

25 g (1 oz) cashew nuts

salt and freshly ground black pepper

1 teaspoon sesame seeds, to garnish

1 In a small bowl or jug, mix together the soy sauce, honey, vinegar, chilli sauce and cornflour.

2 Put the noodles in a bowl and cover with boiling water. Soak them for about 6 minutes, or according to the pack instructions.

3 Heat a non stick omelette pan or large non stick frying pan and lightly spray it with low fat cooking spray. Beat the eggs and milk together and pour into the pan, and cook until just set. Fold the omelette over, turn it out on to a warm plate and keep warm.

4 Heat the stir fry oil or sesame oil in a wok or large frying pan, and add the garlic, ginger and stir fry vegetables. Stir fry briskly for about 3 minutes and then add the hot, drained noodles.

5 Stir the soy sauce mixture to blend the ingredients, and then add it to

the vegetable mixture, tossing to coat everything.

6 Slice the omelette into fine shreds and add it to the pan or wok, stir frying for about 1 minute to reheat it. Add the cashew nuts and season with a little salt and pepper. Serve, on four warmed plates sprinkled with sesame seeds.

Top tip You can buy ready prepared fresh or frozen No Point stir fry vegetables – or simply prepare your own No Point choice. Celery, cucumber, spring onions, Chinese leaves or pak choi, carrots and mushrooms work well together.

Variation For a chicken version, add 175 g (6 oz) of chopped, cooked chicken to the pan with the hot drained noodles and reheat thoroughly. The Points will be 5 per serving.

1 Cook the pasta shapes for about 8–10 minutes in plenty of boiling, lightly salted water, or according to pack instructions, until just tender.

2 Meanwhile, lightly spray a large saucepan with low fat cooking spray and sauté the spring onions for about 3 minutes, until softened. Add the asparagus, courgette and frozen petit pois or garden peas. Cook, stirring, for 2–3 minutes.

3 Add the fromage frais, soft cheese, lemon zest and torn mint leaves to the pan. Cook gently for about 4 minutes, stirring from time to time. Season with salt and pepper.

4 Drain the pasta, reserving 2 tablespoons of the cooking liquid, and then return it with the reserved liquid to the saucepan. Add the sauce to the pasta, mixing it in gently.

5 Transfer the pasta mixture to four warmed plates and sprinkle each portion with 1 teaspoon of Parmesan cheese. Serve, garnished with mint leaves and the lemon wedge.

Top tip You don't have to use penne – any pasta shape will work well. The Points will stay the same.

Variation If asparagus is too expensive or not in season, use fine green beans instead. The Points will remain the same.

Pasta Primavera: Delicious springtime flavours for 5½ Points.

PASTA PRIMAVERA

5½ POINTS

21½ Points per recipe

v Serves 4

Preparation and cooking time: 40 minutes

Calories per serving: 335

Freezing: recommended

Literally meaning 'springtime pasta', this classic Italian dish is bursting with the new season's flavours. Make sure that the vegetables are really fresh for the very best result.

225 g (8 oz) penne

low fat cooking spray

1 bunch of spring onions, chopped

100 g (3½ oz) fine asparagus spears, sliced

1 courgette, chopped

75 g (2¾ oz) frozen petit pois or garden peas

100 ml (3½ fl oz) very low fat plain fromage frais

250 g tub of low fat soft cheese with garlic and herbs

finely grated zest of 1 lemon

a few mint leaves, torn into shreds

4 teaspoons Parmesan cheese

salt and freshly ground black pepper

SPINACH AND POTATO DAHL

3 POINTS

11½ Points per recipe

Ⓥ Serves 4

Preparation time: 20 minutes

Cooking time: 40–45 minutes

Calories per serving: 255

Freezing: recommended

Potatoes and spinach taste so good together in this easy Indian spiced curry.

low fat cooking spray

1 teaspoon cumin seeds

1 large onion, sliced

2 garlic cloves, crushed

1 large fresh green chilli, de-seeded and sliced thinly

1 teaspoon ground coriander

50 g (1¾ oz) dried, split red lentils

700 g (1 lb 9 oz) potatoes, peeled and cut into 2.5 cm (1 inch) cubes

400 g can of chopped tomatoes

1 vegetable stock cube, dissolved in 425 ml (15 fl oz) hot water

500 g (1lb 2 oz) fresh spinach leaves, washed thoroughly

salt and freshly ground black pepper

To serve

4 tablespoons low fat plain yogurt

coriander sprigs (optional)

1 Spray a large saucepan with low fat cooking spray. Add the cumin seeds, onion and garlic and sauté them over a low heat for about 4–5 minutes, until the onion has softened.

2 Add the chilli, coriander, lentils and potato cubes and cook, stirring, for another 2–3 minutes. Tip in the canned tomatoes and stir well.

3 Pour the stock into the saucepan and bring to the boil. Lower the heat and simmer gently for 40–45 minutes, until the lentils and potatoes are tender.

4 Pack the spinach into a separate saucepan and cook, covered, for 4–5 minutes to wilt the leaves. Drain really well, squeezing out the excess moisture. Chop the spinach roughly and then stir it into the potato mixture. Cook for another couple of minutes and then season with salt and pepper.

5 Serve each portion of the dahl with 1 tablespoon of yogurt and garnish with the coriander sprigs, if using.

Top tip There's no need to add any water to the saucepan when you cook spinach, as the water left on the leaves from washing it will be enough to wilt the leaves.

Spinach and Potato Dahl: An authentic Indian dish for only 3 Points.

Spinach and Feta
Pastries: A Greek
treat for only 2
Points per serving.

SPINACH AND FETA PASTRIES

2 POINTS

13½ Points per recipe

Ⓥ Serves 6

Preparation time: 20 minutes

Cooking time: 30–35 minutes

Calories per serving: 165

Freezing: recommended

These tasty Greek pastries are delicious eaten on their own for a snack or a packed lunch, or serve them with a No Point salad or No Point vegetables for a more substantial meal.

750 g (1 lb 10 oz) fresh spinach leaves, washed thoroughly

low fat cooking spray

1 medium onion, chopped finely

1 garlic clove, crushed

2 teaspoons Italian mixed dried herbs

1 egg, beaten

6 sheets of filo pastry, defrosted if frozen

100 g (3½ oz) feta cheese, crumbled

salt and freshly ground black pepper

1 Preheat the oven to Gas Mark 6/200°C/fan oven 180°C.

2 Pack the spinach into a large saucepan and cook, without adding any water, for 3–4 minutes until the leaves have wilted. Drain well, squeezing out any excess moisture with the back of a spoon. Cool and chop roughly.

3 Heat a non stick frying pan and spray it with low fat cooking spray. Add the onion and garlic, and sauté them gently for 3–4 minutes, until softened. Allow to cool, and then mix in the herbs, egg and spinach. Season with salt and pepper.

4 Lightly spray a baking sheet or Swiss roll tin with low fat cooking spray. Lay 1 sheet of filo pastry on top and lightly spray it with low fat cooking spray. If the pastry sheet is too big, just fold in the edges. Repeat the process with 2 more sheets of filo pastry. Spoon on the filling, spreading it out evenly, and then sprinkle the feta cheese over the top.

5 Lay the remaining pastry sheets over the filling, spraying them with low fat cooking spray as before, and then spray the surface.

6 Bake for 30–35 minutes, until the pastry is golden. Cool for a few minutes, and then cut into six portions.

Top tip Keep filo pastry covered with clingfilm or a damp tea towel as you work to prevent it drying out.

CHICK PEA BALTI

6 POINTS

12 Points per recipe

Ⓥ Serves 2

Preparation time: 25 minutes

Cooking time: 20–25 minutes

Calories per serving: 360

Freezing: recommended

This is one of the best meals to make when you're feeling really hungry and in need of a hearty plateful of food. The bonus is that it's still low in Points and very good for you.

low fat cooking spray

1 medium onion, sliced

1 garlic clove, crushed

100 g (3½ oz) sweet potatoes, peeled and chopped

1 courgette, sliced

1 carrot, sliced

1 small red or green pepper, de-seeded and chopped

100 g (3½ oz) cauliflower florets

50 g (1¾ oz) fine green beans, sliced

1½ tablespoons balti curry paste

400 g can of chopped tomatoes

410 g can of chick peas, drained and rinsed

1 vegetable stock cube dissolved in 300 ml (10 fl oz) boiling water

1 tablespoon chopped fresh coriander

2 teaspoons cornflour, blended with 2 tablespoons cold water

salt and freshly ground black pepper

To serve

2 tablespoons low fat plain yogurt

sprigs of fresh coriander

1 Heat the low fat cooking spray in a very large saucepan. Sauté the onion for 3–4 minutes and then add the garlic and cook for 1 more minute.

2 Add all the vegetables, curry paste, canned tomatoes, chick peas and stock. Cook until just boiling and then reduce the heat. Cover and simmer for 20–25 minutes, until all the vegetables are tender.

3 Add the chopped coriander and blended cornflour to the saucepan, stirring until the sauce is thickened. Taste the curry, adding salt and pepper, if needed.

4 Serve the curry in two warmed bowls, topped with 1 tablespoon of yogurt per portion and coriander sprigs.

Variations Vary the No Point vegetables when making this curry.

For a more substantial meal, serve each portion with 4 tablespoons of boiled rice for an extra 3 Points per serving.

VEGETABLE CHOW MEIN

13 Points per recipe

Ⓥ Serves 4

*Preparation and cooking time:
25 minutes + 1–2 hours marinating
Calories per serving: 285
Freezing: not recommended*

Egg noodles only take a few minutes to prepare, so combine them with stir fried vegetables to make a quick and tasty Chinese style supper.

3 tablespoons light soy sauce

1 tablespoon rice vinegar or white wine vinegar

1 large fresh green chilli, de-seeded and sliced finely

1 teaspoon finely grated fresh root ginger

2 tablespoons chopped fresh coriander or parsley

1 teaspoon Chinese five spice powder

250 g (9 oz) firm tofu, cubed

175 g (6 oz) medium egg noodles

2 teaspoons stir fry oil or vegetable oil

1 bunch of spring onions, chopped

1 carrot, cut into fine strips

3 celery sticks, chopped

¼ cucumber, de-seeded and sliced

75 g (2¾ oz) fresh beansprouts

salt and freshly ground black pepper

sprigs of fresh coriander or parsley, to garnish

1 Put the soy sauce, vinegar, chilli, ginger, coriander or parsley and five spice powder into a non metallic bowl. Stir well and then add the tofu cubes. Cover and leave to marinate for 1–2 hours, or overnight if preferred.

2 Soak the egg noodles in boiling water for about 6 minutes, or according to the pack instructions.

3 Heat the oil in a wok or large frying pan and add the spring onions, carrot, celery and cucumber. Stir fry for 2–3 minutes. Add the tofu with its marinade and then the beansprouts. Stir fry for another 2 minutes.

4 Drain the noodles thoroughly and add them to the wok or pan. Stir fry them for about 2 minutes to heat them through. Season to taste and serve, garnished with sprigs of fresh coriander or parsley.

VEGETABLE CHILLI

19½ Points per recipe

Ⓥ Ⓥg Serves 4

*Preparation time: 15 minutes
Cooking time: 30 minutes
Calories per serving: 375
Freezing: recommended*

Bring the flavours of Mexico to your table with this easy to make tasty vegetarian chilli.

low fat cooking spray

1 large onion, chopped

2 garlic cloves, crushed

3 celery sticks, chopped finely

1 large carrot, chopped finely

1 courgette, chopped

350 g pack of Quorn mince

2–3 teaspoons medium chilli powder

400 g can of chopped tomatoes

2 tablespoons tomato purée

215 g can of red kidney beans, rinsed and drained

198 g can of sweetcorn with peppers

1 vegetable stock cube, dissolved in 300 ml (10 fl oz) boiling water

175 g (6 oz) long grain rice

salt and freshly ground black pepper

1 Heat a large saucepan and spray it with low fat cooking spray. Add the onion, garlic, celery, carrot and courgette. Stir fry for 2–3 minutes.

2 Add the Quorn mince, chilli powder, tomatoes, tomato purée, red kidney beans, sweetcorn with peppers and stock to the pan. Stir well and bring to the boil. Cover, reduce the heat and simmer for about 30 minutes, stirring from time to time.

3 15 minutes before you're ready to serve, put the rice on to cook in plenty of lightly salted, boiling water.

Cook for about 12 minutes, until tender. Drain well and rinse with boiling water.

4 Check the seasoning of the chilli, adding salt and pepper according to taste. Divide the cooked rice between four serving plates and pile the cooked chilli on top. Serve at once.

Top tips Cook spicy food according your taste, adding extra chilli powder if you like things spicy, or use it sparingly if you prefer a milder flavour.

Green Giant sell cans of sweetcorn with peppers and they are available in supermarkets. Although not as quick, you could also use 150 g (5½ oz) sweetcorn and 50 g (1¾ oz) chopped peppers. The Points per serving will then be 4½

MUSHROOM RISOTTO

5½ POINTS

11 Points per recipe

Ⓥ *Serves 2*

Preparation and cooking time:
40 minutes

Calories per serving: 330

Freezing: not recommended

The secret of a successful risotto is to choose the right variety of rice, and then be patient as it slowly absorbs the stock to become creamy and delicious.

15 g (½ oz) sun dried tomatoes
2 teaspoons olive oil
100 g (3½ oz) arborio or risotto rice
1 small onion, chopped
1 small garlic clove, crushed
1 celery stick, sliced
½ red or yellow pepper, de-seeded and chopped
175 g (6 oz) mixed mushrooms, sliced
50 ml (2 fl oz) dry white wine
1 vegetable stock cube dissolved in 425 ml (15 fl oz) hot water
1 tablespoon chopped fresh herbs (basil, oregano, marjoram, chives or parsley)
2 tablespoons finely grated Parmesan cheese
salt and freshly ground black pepper

1 Put the tomatoes in a bowl and pour over enough boiling water to just cover them. Leave them to soak for 20 minutes.

2 Meanwhile, heat the oil in a heavy based frying pan or saucepan. Add the rice and gently sauté it, without browning, for about 5 minutes. Add the onion, garlic, celery, pepper and mushrooms. Cook over a very low heat, stirring, for 2–3 more minutes.

3 Pour in the wine, allowing it to bubble up for a few moments, and then add about a quarter of the hot stock and bring to the boil. Reduce the heat and simmer gently, stirring occasionally, for about 10 minutes. Ladle in more stock as needed and cook until the rice is almost tender.

4 Drain the tomatoes, adding the soaking liquid to the rice. Tear the tomatoes into pieces and add them to the risotto with any remaining stock. Cook gently until the liquid has been absorbed and the rice is tender.

5 Add the herbs and half the Parmesan cheese to the risotto. Season with salt and pepper and serve at once, sprinkled with the remaining cheese.

Top tip Add a little extra stock or water if the rice is not fully cooked after it has absorbed all the liquid.

Variation Leave the pepper out if you're not keen on its flavour, or replace it with a chopped courgette. The Points will remain the same.

Mushroom Risotto: Filling and comforting but only 5½ Points.

**Vegetable Enchiladas:
Enjoy great Mexican
food for 5½ Points.**

VEGETABLE ENCHILADAS

21¹⁄₂ Points per recipe

Ⓥ Serves 4

Preparation time: 20 minutes

Cooking time: 20–25 minutes

Calories per serving: 310

Freezing: recommended before baking

Mexican style soft tortillas are used in this easy recipe. They are available from most supermarkets and delicatessens, so do try them in this excellent vegetarian dish.

---

low fat cooking spray

1 onion, chopped

1–2 garlic cloves, crushed

1 red pepper, de-seeded and chopped

1 small aubergine, chopped

100 g (3¹⁄₂ oz) mushrooms, sliced

400 g can of chick peas, drained and rinsed

---

1 teaspoon mild chilli powder

2 tablespoons tomato purée

2 tablespoons chopped fresh coriander

4 soft flour tortillas

100 g (3¹⁄₂ oz) half fat Cheddar cheese, grated

salt and freshly ground black pepper

sprigs of fresh coriander, to garnish (optional)

---

1 Preheat the oven to Gas Mark 4/ 180°C/fan oven 160°C. Spray a 1.5 litre (2¾ pint) baking dish with low fat cooking spray.

2 Heat a large frying pan and spray it with low fat cooking spray. Add the onion, garlic, pepper, aubergine and mushrooms, and sauté them for about 5 minutes, until softened.

3 Add the chick peas and chilli powder to the pan. Cook for about 5 minutes, stirring often. Stir in the tomato purée and coriander. Season with salt and pepper. Remove from the heat.

4 Lay the tortillas on a work surface and divide the filling equally between them. Roll them up and place them in the baking dish. Scatter the grated cheese on top and bake in the oven for 20–25 minutes.

5 Serve the tortillas, garnished with sprigs of fresh coriander, if using.

Variation Instead of the chick peas, use 175 g (6 oz) of canned or frozen sweetcorn. The Points per serving will be 4.

Top tip Why not serve a No Point home made salsa with the enchiladas? Just mix together finely chopped red onion, cucumber, tomatoes, coriander or parsley. Flavour it with lime juice, chilli sauce, salt and pepper.

SPINACH AND CHEESE CANNELLONI

30¹⁄₂ Points per recipe

Ⓥ Serves 4

Preparation time: 20 minutes

Cooking time: 25–30 minutes

Calories per serving: 415

Freezing: recommended

It's so easy to make this delicious cannelloni with its tasty filling of spinach and soft cheese.

---

450 g (1 lb) fresh spinach leaves, washed thoroughly

250 g tub of low fat soft cheese with garlic and herbs

low fat cooking spray

500 g jar of tomato pasta sauce with basil

---

225 g (8 oz) no pre cook cannelloni tubes

4 tablespoons finely grated Parmesan cheese

salt and freshly ground black pepper

fresh basil leaves, to garnish

---

1 Preheat the oven to Gas Mark 4/ 180°C/fan oven 160°C.

2 Pack the spinach into a very large saucepan. Cover and cook for about 4 minutes, until the leaves have wilted. You don't need to add any water, as the spinach will cook in the water left clinging to the leaves after washing. Drain well, squeezing out the excess moisture. Cool and chop.

3 Put the soft cheese into a mixing bowl. Add the spinach, mix well and season with salt and pepper.

4 Lightly spray a shallow ovenproof dish with low fat cooking spray.

Spoon about one third of the tomato pasta sauce over the base of the dish. Using a teaspoon, fill the cannelloni tubes with the spinach mixture and then arrange them in the baking dish. Pour the remaining pasta sauce over the cannelloni tubes. Sprinkle over half of the Parmesan cheese.

5 Bake for 25–30 minutes, until bubbling and browned. Sprinkle with the remaining Parmesan cheese and serve at once, garnished with basil leaves.

Top tip Make sure that you buy cannelloni tubes that do not require pre-cooking.

Variation When fresh spinach is not available, use frozen leaf spinach instead.

fish
main courses

This chapter shows you how to prepare lots of exciting fish recipes – and they're so easy to make too. Fish cooks exceptionally quickly – it really is the original fast food. So choose it and use it in preference to instant foods and ready meals. It's so good for you – you'll be doing your health a favour!

PAELLA

5 POINTS

29½ Points per recipe
Serves 6
Preparation time: 20 minutes
Cooking time: 45 minutes
Calories per serving: 345
Freezing: recommended

The name 'paella' actually refers to the large, flat cooking pan in which this famous Spanish fish recipe is cooked. It's one of the great dishes of the world.

a pinch of saffron strands

2 fish or chicken stock cubes, dissolved in 1.2 litres (2 pints) boiling water

low fat cooking spray

2 garlic cloves, crushed

1 bunch of spring onions, chopped finely

1 medium red pepper, de-seeded and chopped

350 g (12 oz) arborio or risotto rice

225 g (8 oz) squid rings

350 g (12 oz) cooked prawns in shells

450 g (1 lb) fresh mussels, scrubbed

2 tablespoons chopped fresh parsley

1 bay leaf

125 ml (4 fl oz) dry white wine

1 tablespoon lemon juice

50 g (1¾ oz) frozen petit pois or garden peas

salt and freshly ground black pepper

lemon wedges and chopped fresh parsley, to garnish

1 Add the saffron strands to the hot stock and let them infuse for 10–15 minutes.
2 Heat a wok or large frying pan and spray it with low fat cooking spray. Add the garlic, spring onions and red pepper. Sauté them for about 5 minutes until softened.
3 Add the rice to the wok or frying pan and sauté for 1 minute. Pour in the saffron infused hot stock and bring to the boil. Reduce the heat and simmer for 10 minutes.

4 Add all the remaining ingredients, apart from the garnish, and stir well. Cook gently, uncovered, for about 20 minutes, stirring occasionally, until the liquid has been absorbed and the rice is tender. Add a little extra liquid if it has all been absorbed before the rice is cooked.
5 Discard the bay leaf and any mussels that have not opened during cooking. Season well with salt and pepper and then serve, garnished with lemon wedges and parsley.

Top tip When preparing fresh mussels, be sure to discard any that are damaged, or remain open when tapped.

Variation To make a chicken paella, replace the squid and mussels with 350 g (12 oz) of chopped, cooked chicken 10 minutes before the end of the cooking time. The Points per serving will be 5½.

Paella: A mouthwatering medley of flavours for only 5 Points per serving.

Salmon en Croûte:
Enjoy with new
potatoes for 8 Points.

SALMON EN CROUTE

7 POINTS

28 Points per recipe

Serves 4

Preparation time: 20 minutes

Cooking time: 30–35 minutes

Calories per serving: 395

Freezing: recommended

Fresh salmon fillets wrapped and baked in sheets of filo pastry make a really special meal. Serve with fresh asparagus or fine green beans and 100 g (3½ oz) new potatoes, adding 1 extra Point per serving.

low fat cooking spray

6 sheets filo pastry, defrosted if frozen

2 tablespoons plain white flour

4 × 140 g (5 oz) fresh salmon fillets (do not use steaks)

60 g (2 oz) low fat soft cheese with garlic and herbs

finely grated zest of 1 lemon

4 teaspoons chopped fresh dill or parsley

salt and freshly ground black pepper

1 Preheat the oven to Gas Mark 4/ 180°C/fan oven 160°C. Lightly spray a baking sheet with low fat cooking spray.

2 Take 1 sheet of filo pastry, spray it 3–4 times with low fat cooking spray and then lay another sheet on top. Spray the second sheet in the same way, and then place a third sheet on top and spray yet again. Cut this stack in half widthways. Repeat the process with the remaining 3 sheets to give you four piles of filo pastry.

3 Sprinkle the flour on to a plate and season with salt and pepper.

Rinse the salmon fillets and pat them dry with kitchen paper. Check that there are no bones in them and then dip them in the flour, patting off any excess flour.

4 Place a piece of floured fish in the middle of each pile of pastry and then spoon an equal amount of soft cheese on top of each fillet. Spread it over the surface and sprinkle the lemon zest and herbs on top. Season lightly.

5 Fold the filo pastry over the fillets to make parcels, tucking in the ends. Lift the parcels on to the baking sheet and lightly spray them with low fat cooking spray. Bake them in the oven for 30–35 minutes, until the pastry is golden.

Variation Try using trout fillets or sea bass. The Points will be 5 and 4 respectively.

SEAFOOD PROVENCAL

5½ POINTS

22½ Points per recipe

Serves 4

Preparation time: 15 minutes

Cooking time: 30–35 minutes

Calories per serving: 425

Freezing: recommended

You'll love the robust flavours of this soupy fish stew. It will transport your tastebuds to the south of France!

1 tablespoon olive oil

1 large onion, sliced

1 large courgette, sliced

1 bulb of fennel or 3 celery sticks, chopped

2 garlic cloves, crushed

1 medium aubergine, chopped

50 ml (2 fl oz) dry white wine

2 × 400 g cans of chopped tomatoes

2 teaspoons dried Herbes de Provence or mixed dried herbs

1 vegetable stock cube dissolved in 150 ml (5 fl oz) boiling water

450 g (1 lb) cod, cut into chunks

175 g (6 oz) large peeled prawns, defrosted if frozen

1 tablespoon cornflour blended with 2–3 tablespoons cold water

salt and freshly ground black pepper

2 tablespoons chopped fresh flat leaf parsley

4 × 60 g (2 oz) slices French bread

1 Heat the oil in a large saucepan and add the onion, courgette, fennel or celery, garlic and aubergine. Sauté them for 4–5 minutes, until softened.

2 Pour in the wine and let it bubble up for a few moments. Add the tomatoes, dried herbs and stock, and bring to the boil. Reduce the heat and simmer for 20 minutes, until the vegetables are tender.

3 Add the fish to the pan and cook for 3–4 minutes. Mix in the prawns and cook for another 2 minutes. Stir the cornflour mixture and add it to the pan, stirring gently. Cook for another 2 minutes, until the liquid is slightly thickened.

4 Taste, adding salt and pepper as required. Ladle into four warmed soup plates or bowls, and garnish with chopped fresh parsley. Serve each with a slice of crusty French bread.

Variation Try replacing the cod with monkfish. The Points will remain the same.

MOULES MARINIERES

3 Points per recipe
Serves 1
Preparation and cooking time:
30 minutes
Calories per serving: 230
Freezing: not recommended

A classic French recipe. Serve with a 60 g (2 oz) slice of French bread to mop up the juices, adding an extra 2½ Points.

---

350 g (12 oz) mussels
1 teaspoon olive oil
2 spring onions, chopped finely
1 garlic clove, chopped finely
50 ml (2 fl oz) dry white wine
½ fish or vegetable stock cube, dissolved in 50 ml (2 fl oz) boiling water
1 small tomato, skinned and chopped
freshly ground black pepper
1 tablespoon chopped fresh parsley, to garnish

---

1 Scrub the mussels with a small stiff brush and scrape away their beards with a sharp knife. Throw away any damaged mussels or ones that remain open when tapped.

2 Heat the oil in a large saucepan. Sauté the spring onions and garlic for about 3 minutes, until softened. Add the wine, stock and tomato, and heat until bubbling. Now tip in the mussels.

3 Cover and cook for 3–4 minutes, until the shells have opened. Discard any mussels that remain shut.

4 Serve the mussels with the wine and garlic pan juices, seasoned with black pepper and garnished with the chopped fresh parsley.

THAI FISH CURRY

12 Points per recipe
Serves 4
Preparation time: 25–30 minutes
Cooking time: 20–25 minutes
Calories per serving: 225
Freezing: recommended

Thousands of miles of coastline surround Thailand, so it's no surprise that fish curries are so popular there.

---

low fat cooking spray
6 shallots or 1 large onion, sliced
1 garlic clove, sliced thinly
200 ml (7 fl oz) reduced fat coconut milk
1 vegetable stock cube, dissolved in 425 ml (15 fl oz) boiling water
3–4 teaspoons Thai green curry paste
350 g (12 oz) butternut squash, peeled, de-seeded and cut into chunks
1 red pepper, de-seeded and cut into chunks
125 g (4½ oz) fine green beans, halved
2 tablespoons chopped fresh coriander
1 tablespoon Thai fish sauce or light soy sauce
1 teaspoon ready prepared 'fresh' ginger
1 teaspoon ready prepared 'fresh' lemongrass
1 fresh green chilli, de-seeded and sliced thinly (optional)
200 g (7 oz) haddock
200 g (7 oz) cooked large tiger prawns, with tails, defrosted if frozen
salt and freshly ground black pepper
sprigs of fresh coriander, to garnish

---

1 Heat a large sauté pan or wok and lightly spray it with low fat cooking spray. Add the shallots or onion and garlic and cook over a medium heat for about 4–5 minutes, until softened.

2 Add all the remaining ingredients, apart from the haddock, prawns and coriander. Bring to the boil. Reduce the heat and simmer gently for about 20–25 minutes, until the butternut squash is tender.

3 Add the fish to the pan and cook for 2–3 minutes. Add the prawns and cook for another 2–3 minutes. Check the seasoning, adding salt and pepper, if needed.

4 Ladle the curry into four bowls and serve, garnished with sprigs of fresh coriander.

Top tip Remember that curries have to be cooked according to your own taste, so it's better to add a little curry paste at first if you're not sure how hot you want it to be. You can always add a little more as you go.

Variation For a virtually vegetarian version, leave out the fish and prawns. Add extra No Point vegetables, such as more peppers, courgettes and mushrooms. Make sure that you use soy sauce, not fish sauce. Remember that most varieties of Thai curry paste include dried shrimp in the ingredients. The Points per serving will be 2.

Thai Fish Curry:
A deliciously
fragrant dish
and only 3
Points!

1 Preheat the oven to Gas Mark 5/ 190°C/fan oven 170°C.

2 Pack the spinach into a large saucepan and cook, without adding any water, for 3–4 minutes until the leaves have wilted. Drain well, squeezing out any excess moisture with the back of a spoon. Cool and chop roughly.

3 Lightly spray a 1 litre (1¾ pint) baking dish with low fat cooking spray. Spread the spinach over the base and then top with the sliced tomatoes. Season and then lay the sole fillets on top. Season once more and sprinkle over the lemon juice.

4 Place the soft cheese, fromage frais and Cheddar cheese in a small saucepan and heat gently, stirring until combined. Spread this sauce evenly over the fish.

5 Sprinkle the surface with breadcrumbs and Parmesan cheese, and then transfer to the oven. Bake for 30–35 minutes. Serve garnished with parsley.

Top tip For a hint of garlic, choose low fat soft cheese flavoured with garlic and herbs. The Points will remain the same.

Variation Try making this dish with coley instead of lemon sole. The Points per serving will remain the same.

Sole Florentine: A wonderful combination of flavours for just 4 Points.

SOLE FLORENTINE

4 POINTS

7½ Points per recipe

Serves 2

Preparation time: 15 minutes

Cooking time: 30–35 minutes

Calories per serving: 240

Freezing: recommended

This Mediterranean recipe for sole fillets cooked with spinach, tomatoes and low fat soft cheese sauce is so easy and quick to make. Delicious served alone, or with plenty of No Point vegetables.

250 g (9 oz) fresh spinach leaves, washed thoroughly

low fat cooking spray

2 tomatoes, skinned and sliced

250 g (9 oz) lemon sole fillets

a few drops of lemon juice

60 g (2 oz) low fat soft cheese

3 tablespoons very low fat plain fromage frais

15 g (½ oz) half fat mature Cheddar cheese, grated finely

1 tablespoon fresh white breadcrumbs

1 tablespoon finely grated Parmesan cheese

salt and freshly ground black pepper

parsley sprigs, to garnish

THAI FISH CAKES

17 Points per recipe

Serves 4
Preparation time: 20 minutes
Cooking time: 25–30 minutes
Calories per serving: 225
Freezing: recommended

Crab cakes are a Thai speciality – and no wonder, as they taste so good. Serve them with a No Point vegetable stir fry, or with salad.

2 teaspoons sesame or stir fry oil
75 g (2³/₄ oz) long grain rice
3 shallots or 1 small onion, chopped
1 large garlic clove, crushed
2 tablespoons chopped fresh coriander
170 g can of crabmeat, drained
1 tablespoon Thai fish sauce or light soy sauce
200 ml (7 fl oz) reduced fat coconut milk
2 eggs, beaten
2 teaspoons Thai red curry paste
salt and freshly ground black pepper
spring onions, red chillies and sprigs of fresh coriander, to garnish

1 Preheat the oven to Gas Mark 4/ 180°C/fan oven 160°C. Grease four 200 ml (7 fl oz) ramekins with ½ teaspoon of the oil.
2 Cook the rice in plenty of lightly salted, boiling water for about 12 minutes, until just tender. Rinse with cold water and drain well.
3 Heat the remaining oil in a small frying pan and sauté the shallots or onion and garlic for about 5 minutes, until softened and golden brown.
4 In a large bowl, mix together the rice, shallots or onion, garlic, coriander, crab, fish sauce or soy sauce, coconut milk, eggs and curry paste. Season.
5 Divide the mixture between the dishes. Bake for 25–30 minutes, until set.
6 Leave to cool slightly, then turn them out and serve, garnished with finely sliced spring onions, red chilli and fresh coriander.

INDIAN FISH CURRY

17½ Points per recipe

Serves 4
Preparation time: 20 minutes
Cooking time: 20 minutes
Calories per serving: 315
Freezing: recommended

A wonderful, fragrant fish curry.

500 g (1 lb 2 oz) tuna steaks, defrosted if frozen
low fat cooking spray
1 large onion, sliced
1 garlic clove, crushed
1 medium courgette, sliced
3 medium tomatoes, skinned and chopped
1 small aubergine, chopped
400 g can of chopped tomatoes
400 g can of chick peas, drained and rinsed
1 teaspoon ground cumin
1 tablespoon chopped fresh coriander
2 tablespoons mild curry paste
salt and freshly ground black pepper

To serve
fresh coriander sprigs
4 lime or lemon wedges

1 Rinse the fish and then chop into large chunks, and set aside.
2 Heat a large frying pan or wok and spray with the low fat cooking spray. Add the onion and garlic and sauté over a medium heat for 2 minutes. Add the courgette, fresh tomatoes and aubergine, and cook, stirring, for a further 2–3 minutes.
3 Add the canned tomatoes, chick peas, cumin, chopped coriander and curry paste. Stir well and bring to the boil. Reduce the heat and simmer for 15 minutes.
4 Add the fish chunks and stir them in gently. Cook for another 5–6 minutes, until the fish is cooked and looks opaque. Taste, adding salt and pepper, if needed.
5 Ladle the fish curry into four serving bowls and garnish with coriander sprigs. Serve with the lime or lemon wedges.

Top tip Serve the curry with 4 tablespoons of boiled rice, adding 3 extra Points.

Variation Try replacing the tuna with swordfish. The Points per serving will remain the same.

PRAWN LAKSA

21½ Points per recipe

Serves 4

Preparation and cooking time:
30 minutes

Calories per serving: 295

Freezing: not recommended

This Malaysian soup is very popular throughout Southeast Asia.

125 g (4½ oz) rice noodles

low fat cooking spray

4 shallots, sliced

2 teaspoons ready prepared 'fresh' lemongrass

2 teaspoons finely grated fresh root ginger

200 ml (7 fl oz) reduced fat coconut milk

200 ml (7 fl oz) vegetable stock

3–4 teaspoons Thai red curry paste

1 tablespoon Thai fish sauce or light soy sauce

450 g (1 lb) large peeled prawns, defrosted if frozen

1 tablespoon chopped fresh coriander

finely sliced red chillies and chopped fresh coriander, to garnish

1 Put the rice noodles into a bowl, cover them with boiling water and soak for 4 minutes.

2 Meanwhile, lightly spray a wok or large frying pan with low fat cooking spray and sauté the shallots for about 3 minutes, until softened. Add the lemongrass, ginger, coconut milk, stock, curry paste and fish sauce or soy sauce. Heat until almost boiling.

3 Add the prawns to the wok or frying pan with the chopped coriander and cook gently for 2 minutes. Add the drained noodles and cook for a further 2 minutes, until they are heated through.

4 Serve the laksa in four warmed, shallow bowls, garnished with sliced chillies and coriander.

CHILLI PRAWN KEBABS

12 Points per recipe

Serves 4

Preparation and cooking time:
20 minutes + 30 minutes marinating

Calories per serving: 220

Freezing: not recommended

Ideal for a summertime barbecue.

1 tablespoon sesame or stir fry oil

3 tablespoons soy sauce

2 tablespoons lime or lemon juice

1 tablespoon chopped fresh mint or coriander

1 teaspoon finely grated fresh root ginger or ready prepared 'fresh' ginger

2 tablespoons hot chilli sauce

½ teaspoon Chinese five spice powder

1 red or yellow pepper, de-seeded and cut into chunks

1 courgette, sliced

350 g (12 oz) large peeled prawns, defrosted if frozen

350 g (12 oz) firm tofu, cut into chunks

salt and freshly ground black pepper

lime or lemon wedges and sprigs of mint or coriander, to garnish (optional)

1 In a shallow, non metallic dish, mix together the oil, soy sauce, lime or lemon juice, mint or coriander, ginger, chilli sauce, five spice powder and seasoning. Soak twelve wooden kebab sticks in water for 10 minutes.

2 Thread the vegetables, prawns and tofu evenly on to the twelve wooden kebab sticks and then lay them in the marinade, turning to coat them on all sides. Cover and leave to marinate for at least 30 minutes, turning occasionally.

3 Preheat the grill. Arrange the kebabs on the grill rack and cook for 4–5 minutes, turning often and basting them with the marinade. Alternatively, cook over barbecue coals in the summer.

4 Serve at once, allowing 3 kebabs per person, garnished with lime or lemon wedges and mint or coriander sprigs, if using.

Chilli Prawn Kebabs: Scrumptious and yet only 3 Points per serving.

**Prawn Laksa:
A Malaysian
dish to wake up
your tastebuds
for 5$\frac{1}{2}$ Points.**

**Summer Pavlova:
For only 3½
Points, what
could be better?**

desserts

Okay, so you're watching your weight, but don't let that stop you enjoying a delicious dessert – in fact, they can be a good way of including more fruit into your diet. Besides, not all puddings are high in Points – and many contain nutrients necessary for our health and well being. That said, we know why desserts are enjoyable... because they taste so good, and that's certainly true of the recipes here!

SUMMER PAVLOVA

36 Points per recipe

Ⓥ *Serves 10*
Preparation time: 25 minutes
Cooking time: 2½–3 hours
Calories per serving: 170
Freezing: recommended

This spectacular creation is the perfect dessert for a summer celebration, although you can make it in winter with frozen berries if fresh ones are not available.

4 large egg whites
200 g (7 oz) caster sugar
200 ml (7 fl oz) whipping cream
225 g (8 oz) strawberries, sliced
225 g (8 oz) raspberries
strawberry leaves or mint leaves, to decorate

1 Preheat the oven to Gas Mark 1/ 140°C/fan oven 120°C. Line a large baking sheet with non stick baking parchment and draw a 25 cm (10 inch) circle on it.
2 In a large grease free bowl and using a hand held electric mixer, whisk the egg whites until they hold their shape. Gradually add the sugar, whisking well, until the egg whites are very stiff and glossy.
3 Spread the meringue in an even layer over the marked out circle. Bake for 2½–3 hours. Remember that the meringue is dried out, rather than cooked, at this low temperature so an exact cooking time isn't necessary. It's a good idea to keep the oven door open just a fraction to get the best possible meringue.

4 Remove the meringue from the oven. Cool it completely and then carefully peel away the baking parchment.
5 When ready to serve, whip the cream until it holds its shape. Pile it on to the meringue and top with the strawberries and raspberries. Decorate with strawberry or mint leaves.

Top tip You can make the meringue base at least a week before you need it. It will store well, either in an airtight tin or wrapped in greaseproof paper.

Variation For a tropical fruit version, use 2 kiwi fruits, 1 medium mango and the juice and pulp from 2 passion fruits. The Points per serving will remain the same.

KEY LIME PIE

41½ Points per recipe

Ⓥ Serves 10

*Preparation time: 15 minutes +
15 minutes chilling
Cooking time: 25 minutes
Calories per serving: 235
Freezing: not recommended*

A slice of pie is a favourite American dessert. This one originates from the Florida Keys, where limes are grown.

60 g (2 oz) polyunsaturated margarine
140 g (5 oz) reduced fat digestive biscuits, crushed
3 eggs, separated
405 g can of skimmed condensed milk
finely grated zest and juice of 3 limes

3–4 drops of green food colouring
25 g (1 oz) caster sugar

1 Melt the margarine in a medium saucepan and add the biscuit crumbs, stirring to coat them all. Tip the coated crumbs into a 23 cm (9 inch) pie or flan dish, pressing them over the base. Chill in the fridge for about 15 minutes.

2 Preheat the oven to Gas Mark 4/ 180°C/fan oven 160°C.

3 Beat the egg yolks and condensed milk together, and then stir in the lime zest and juice. Add a few drops of food colouring to make the mixture pale green. Pour the mixture over the prepared biscuit crumb base and bake for 15–20 minutes, until set.

4 In a grease free bowl and using a perfectly clean whisk or electric beaters, whisk the egg whites until they hold their shape. Add the sugar gradually, whisking well to make stiff, glossy peaks.

5 Pile the meringue mixture on top of the lime pie, spreading it over the surface. Return it to the oven and bake for about 5–6 minutes, until the topping is golden brown.

6 Let the pie cool for about 15 minutes before serving, or you can serve it chilled.

Top tip Egg whites will not whisk successfully if there is the slightest trace of grease, including egg yolk, in the bowl or on the beaters, so make sure everything has just been washed in hot, soapy water before you begin.

PLUM TARTE TATIN

18 Points per recipe

Ⓥ Serves 6

*Preparation time: 30 minutes +
cooling
Cooking time: 25 –30 minutes
Calories per serving: 150
Freezing: not recommended*

This French upside down tart is a real winner. Serve barely warm for the best flavour, accompanied by the chilled half fat crème fraîche.

75 g (2¾ oz) granulated sugar
4 tablespoons just boiled water
500 g (1 lb 2 oz) plums, halved and stoned
4 sheets filo pastry, defrosted if frozen
low fat cooking spray
6 tablespoons half fat crème fraîche, to serve

1 Put the sugar and 3 tablespoons of cold water into a 19–22 cm (7½–8½ inch) heavy based frying pan that will withstand oven temperatures. Cook steadily over a medium heat, without stirring, until the sugar caramelises and turns a rich amber colour. Keep a careful eye on the pan, as the sugar continues to cook and can easily burn.

2 Being very careful, pour the hot water into the pan. The mixture will bubble up, but it will soon settle. If the mixture solidifies, cook over a low heat for 1–2 minutes to make sure that the caramel has melted.

3 Add the plums to the pan, packing them in so they are level with the rim of the pan. Cook over a low heat for 8–10 minutes, so that the plums cook in the caramel sauce. Remove the pan from the heat and cool completely. This will take about 30 minutes.

4 Preheat the oven to Gas Mark 5/ 190°C/fan oven 170°C.

5 Cut the filo pastry sheets in half. Spray each piece of filo with low fat cooking spray and stack them into one pile. Place the stack on top of the frying pan to cover the plums. Trim around the edge, allowing an overhang of about 1 cm (½ inch). Tuck this overlap inside the pan.

6 Stand the pan on a baking sheet and transfer it to the middle shelf of the oven. Bake for 15–20 minutes, until the pastry is light golden brown. Cool for 10 minutes, and then run a knife around the edge to loosen the pastry. Place a large serving plate over the pan – hold it firmly – and invert the pan to release the tart on to the plate.

7 Slice the tarte into six portions. Serve each one with 1 tablespoon of half fat crème fraîche.

Key Lime Pie:
The tasty and
tart American
classic for 4
Points.

Tiramisu with Strawberries: Each delicious dessert has only 3 Points per serving.

TIRAMISU WITH STRAWBERRIES

12½ Points per recipe

Ⓥ Serves 4

Preparation time: 15 minutes + chilling

Calories per serving: 360

Freezing: not recommended

Tiramisu is the classic Italian favourite that literally means 'pick-me-up'. A restaurant version can easily clock up 10 Points or more, that's why it's such a great idea to make your own low Point version.

---

150 ml (5 fl oz) strong coffee, cooled

2 tablespoons amaretto liqueur or Marsala

200 g tub of low fat soft cheese

200 ml (7 fl oz) very low fat plain fromage frais

1 teaspoon vanilla extract

powdered artificial sweetener, to taste

12 sponge fingers

2 teaspoons cocoa powder, for dusting

225 g (8 oz) strawberries, to serve

---

1 In a shallow bowl, mix together the cooled coffee with the amaretto liqueur or Marsala.

2 In another bowl, beat together the soft cheese, fromage frais and vanilla extract until smooth. Add a little sweetener to taste.

3 Dip the sponge fingers briefly into the coffee mixture, layering half of them in the bases of four medium serving glasses or ramekin dishes. Top with half the cheese mixture. Repeat the layers. Cover the desserts and chill them in the fridge until you are ready to serve them.

4 To serve, sprinkle each dessert with half a teaspoon of cocoa powder and serve with the strawberries.

CREME CARAMEL

6 Points per recipe

Ⓥ Serves 2

Preparation time: 10 minutes

Cooking time: 45–50 minutes

Calories per serving: 210

Freezing: not recommended

This perfectly simple, stylish dessert is a real winner. You'll see versions of it throughout Europe, and it's enjoyed everywhere.

---

40 g (1½ oz) granulated sugar

2 small eggs

½ teaspoon vanilla extract

2 teaspoons caster sugar

200 ml (7 fl oz) skimmed milk

---

1 Preheat the oven to Gas Mark 2/ 150°C/fan oven 130°C.

2 Put the granulated sugar and 2 tablespoons of water into a heavy based, medium saucepan and heat gently to dissolve it. Do not stir. Turn up the heat and cook until the sugar begins to caramelise, turning a rich golden colour. Quickly divide this caramel between two ramekin dishes.

3 Break the eggs into a mixing bowl, and beat in the vanilla extract and caster sugar. Pour the milk into the same pan used for the caramel and warm it a little, and then pour it over the egg mixture. Beat together, and then strain this mixture into the dishes.

4 Put the dishes into a roasting pan or baking dish, and pour in enough warm water to come halfway up the sides of the dishes. Transfer to the oven and bake for 45–50 minutes until the crème caramels are set. Cool, and then serve them in the dishes.

CHERRY CLAFOUTIS

12 Points per recipe

Ⓥ Serves 4

Preparation time: 10 minutes

Cooking time: 25–30 minutes

Calories per serving: 210

Freezing: not recommended

This French style hot dessert is wonderfully satisfying. It's a lightly sweetened batter pudding with hot fresh cherries – delicious!

---

low fat cooking spray

110 g (4 oz) plain white flour

a pinch of salt

1 large egg

300 ml (10 fl oz) skimmed milk

1 tablespoon caster sugar

350 g (12 oz) cherries, stoned

2 teaspoons icing sugar, for dusting

---

1 Preheat the oven to Gas Mark 6/ 200°C/fan oven 180°C. Spray four individual baking dishes with low fat cooking spray.

2 Put the flour, salt, egg, milk and sugar into a large mixing bowl, and whisk together to make a smooth batter.

3 Divide the cherries between the baking dishes and pour an equal amount of batter into each one. Transfer the dishes to the oven and bake for 25–30 minutes, until set and golden.

4 Serve at once, dusted with the icing sugar.

Variation When blackberries are in season, try using them instead of cherries. The Points per serving will be 2½.

AMERICAN APPLE PIE

24½ Points per recipe

Ⓥ Serves 8

Preparation time: 20 minutes

Cooking time: 20 minutes

Calories per serving: 160

Freezing: recommended

The warm, spicy flavour of cinnamon gives this American apple pie its distinctive appeal. In this recipe, filo pastry is used to keep the Points to a minimum.

700 g (1 lb 9 oz) cooking apples, peeled, cored and sliced

2 tablespoons lemon juice

½ teaspoon ground cinnamon

75 g (2¾ oz) unrefined caster sugar

low fat cooking spray

8 sheets of filo pastry

2 teaspoons icing sugar, for dusting

8 tablespoons half fat crème fraîche, to serve

1 Put the apples in a large saucepan with the lemon juice, cinnamon and sugar. Add 2 tablespoons of water, and then cover and simmer for 5–8 minutes, until they are tender. Remove from the heat and allow to cool completely.

2 Preheat the oven to Gas Mark 6/ 200°C/fan oven 180°C. Lightly spray a 23 cm (9 inch) pie dish with low fat cooking spray.

3 Line the pie dish with half the pastry sheets, spraying each sheet with low fat cooking spray, and overlapping the edges of the tin slightly. Bake for 4–5 minutes in the centre of the oven.

4 Spoon the cooled apples into the pastry case. Top with the remaining pastry sheets, spraying each sheet 2–3 times with low fat cooking spray. Make loose folds in the pastry so that it fits over the top of the pie dish, and then trim off any excess. Spray the surface another 2–3 times with low fat cooking spray and bake in the oven for 15–20 minutes, until golden.

5 Let the pie cool for a few minutes, and then serve, dusted with the icing sugar and accompanied by the crème fraîche.

Variation Use ground mixed spice instead of the cinnamon, if you prefer. The Points will remain the same.

POTS AU CHOCOLAT

22½ Points per recipe

Ⓥ Serves 6

Preparation and cooking time: 25 minutes + 30 minutes chilling

Calories per serving: 155

Freezing: recommended

These little French chocolate pots are rich and delicious – the perfect finale for a special meal.

60 g (2 oz) plain chocolate, broken into pieces

2 teaspoons unsweetened cocoa powder

4 tablespoons hot water

1 tablespoon caster sugar

2 eggs, separated

100 ml (3½ fl oz) whipping cream

1 Put the chocolate into a small heavy based saucepan with the cocoa powder, hot water and sugar. Heat gently, stirring the mixture constantly until melted and smooth. Do not let the mixture get too hot.

2 Pour the chocolate mixture into a bowl. Add the egg yolks and stir well. Cover the surface with a circle of dampened greaseproof paper to prevent a skin from forming, and cool for about 15 minutes.

3 Whip the cream in a chilled bowl until it holds its shape, and then spoon half of it into the cooled chocolate mixture. Chill the remaining cream.

4 In a grease free bowl and using a very clean whisk or electric beaters, whisk the egg whites until stiff peaks form. Fold them gently into the chocolate mixture. Divide the

mixture between six small pots or serving glasses and chill for at least 30 minutes, or until ready to serve.

5 Just before serving, top each dessert with a spoonful of the reserved cream, to decorate.

Top tip Remember that this recipe contains raw eggs, so it may not be suitable for the very old or young, or for pregnant women.

CHOLOCATE ROULADE

3½ POINTS

22 Points per recipe

Ⓥ Serves 6

Preparation and cooking time:
30 minutes
Calories per serving: 220
Freezing: recommended

Roulade is a wonderful dessert that
looks and tastes indulgent. It's so
simple to make and this version is
unbelievably low in Points.

---

low fat cooking spray

75 g (2 ¾ oz) plain white flour

2 tablespoons unsweetened cocoa
powder

3 large eggs

75 g (2 ¾ oz) unrefined caster sugar

200 g (7 oz) low fat soft cheese

100 ml (3½ fl oz) very low fat
raspberry fromage frais

100 g (3½ oz) raspberries, defrosted
if frozen

2 teaspoons icing sugar, for dusting
mint leaves, to decorate

1 Preheat the oven to Gas Mark 7/
220°C/fan oven 200°C. Spray a 18 cm
x 28 cm (7 inch × 11 inch) Swiss roll
tin with low fat cooking spray and
line it with greaseproof paper. Spray
the paper with low fat cooking spray.
2 Sift the flour and cocoa powder
into a bowl. Set aside.
3 Break the eggs into a large mixing
bowl and add the caster sugar. Use a
hand held electric mixer, whisk them
together until very light and pale in
colour. This will take about 5 minutes.
4 Sift the flour and cocoa mixture
again, this time into the whisked
mixture. Fold it in gently using a
large metal spoon, not a wooden
one. Pour the mixture into the

prepared tin and spread it out to
the corners.
5 Bake in the oven for 7–9 minutes,
until firm yet springy when you
touch it. Turn it out on to a large
sheet of greaseproof paper, and then
carefully peel away the lining paper.
Cover with a clean, damp tea towel
and leave the sponge until cold.
6 Mix together the soft cheese
and fromage frais. Reserve a few
raspberries for decoration, and then
lightly mash the remainder with a
fork. Stir these into the soft cheese
mixture.
7 Trim the edges of the chocolate
sponge, fill with the raspberry
mixture and roll it up. Sprinkle with

icing sugar and serve, decorated
with mint leaves and the reserved
raspberries.

Variation To make a Peach Melba
Roulade, omit the cocoa powder
from the mixture and use a peach
or raspberry flavoured fromage frais,
and add a chopped peach to the
filling. The Points per serving will
remain the same.

Chocolate
Roulade: Treat
yourself for just
3½ Points.

Chocolate Chip Cookies: These just melt in your mouth, for only 2½ Points per serving.

CHOCOLATE CHIP COOKIES

41 Points per recipe

 Makes 16

Preparation time: 10 minutes

Cooking time: 15 minutes

Calories per cookie: 150

Freezing: recommended

Why not make some home made biscuits for those times when you feel like something sweet to nibble. These American style chocolate chip cookies are so good, you'll want to make room for them in your Weight Watchers Programme.

---

low fat cooking spray

110 g (4 oz) polyunsaturated margarine

110 g (4 oz) light muscovado sugar

---

1 egg, beaten

150 g (5½ oz) plain white flour

a pinch of salt

½ teaspoon baking powder

75 g (2¾ oz) rolled oats

50 g (1¾ oz) plain chocolate drops

---

1 Preheat the oven to Gas Mark 4/ 180°C/fan oven 160°C. Spray two baking sheets with low fat cooking spray.

2 Beat the margarine and sugar together in a mixing bowl until it has a light, fluffy texture and is much paler in colour. Beat in the egg, a little at a time.

3 Sift in the flour, salt and baking powder. Add the rolled oats and half the chocolate drops. Stir all the ingredients together until the mixture is combined.

4 Using a tablespoon, place eight heaps of the mixture on to each baking sheet, allowing room for them to spread. Transfer to the oven and bake for 12–15 minutes, until golden.

5 When you take the cookies out of the oven, sprinkle them with the remaining chocolate drops. After a few minutes, transfer the cookies to a wire rack to cool completely.

Variations Use 25 g (1 oz) of chopped hazelnuts instead of the 50 g (1¾ oz) of chocolate drops – the Points per cookie will be 2½. You can use 15 g (½ oz) of both nuts and chocolate drops if you like. The Points will be 2½ per cookie.

LEMON SOUFFLE

4 POINTS

23½ Points per recipe

Serves 6

Preparation time: 25 minutes + 2–3 hours setting

Calories per serving: 205

Freezing: recommended

Light as air lemon soufflé makes the perfect summer dessert, and it's easier to make than you might think.

---

100 ml (3½ fl oz) just boiled water

1 sachet (1 tablespoon) powdered gelatine

3 eggs, separated

110 g (4 oz) caster sugar

finely grated zest and juice of 2 lemons

200 ml (7 fl oz) very low fat plain fromage frais

100 ml (3½ fl oz) whipping cream

lemon slices and mint leaves, to decorate

---

1 Wrap a collar of greaseproof paper or foil around the outside of a 600 ml (1 pint) soufflé dish, so that it extends about 8 cm (3¼ inches) above the rim of the dish. Secure it with string.

2 Pour the just boiled water into a small jug or bowl, sprinkle in the gelatine. Stir and leave it to stand for 3–4 minutes, stirring occasionally, until it is a completely clear liquid. Leave it to cool for 10 minutes.

3 Whisk the egg yolks with the caster sugar, using a hand held electric whisk, until the mixture is very light and pale in colour. This will take about 5 minutes. Whisk in the lemon zest and juice.

4 Beat the fromage frais until smooth and fold it into the lemon mixture. Slowly pour in the cooled gelatine liquid, stirring the mixture as you do so.

5 Whip the cream until it holds its shape and fold it through the mixture.

6 In a very clean bowl and with washed beaters, whisk the egg whites until stiff. Fold them through the lemon mixture. Turn the mixture into the prepared dish and chill in the fridge for about 2–3 hours until set.

7 Carefully remove the paper collar, and then decorate the soufflé with lemon slices and mint leaves.

Top tip It's important to remember that gelatine isn't suitable for vegetarians. Choose a gelatine substitute from a health food store, and follow the pack instructions for its preparation.

CHOCOLATE BROWNIE CAKE

27 Points per recipe

Ⓥ Makes 16 slices

Preparation time: 15 minutes

Cooking time: 25 minutes

Calories per slice: 105

Freezing: recommended

Chocolate brownies are so delicious – and so moreish! Why not make a batch when you're inviting a few friends around, and then freeze any leftover for later.

1 × 225 g (8 oz) cooking apple, peeled, cored and chopped

low fat cooking spray

100 g (3½ oz) self raising white flour

¼ teaspoon salt

60 g (2 oz) unsweetened cocoa powder

1 large egg

2 large egg whites

175 g (6 oz) light muscovado sugar

2 tablespoons vegetable oil

2 teaspoons vanilla extract

1 Cook the apple with 1 tablespoon of water in a covered, small saucepan until very soft. Alternatively, cook it in the microwave on High for 3 minutes, stirring twice. Leave it to go completely cold and then mash it with a fork or potato masher.

2 Preheat the oven to Gas Mark 4/ 180°C/fan oven 160°C. Spray a 23 cm (9 inch) square non stick baking tin with low fat cooking spray and line it with greaseproof paper.

3 Sift the flour, salt and cocoa powder in a bowl. In another large mixing bowl, whisk together the egg and egg whites with the sugar. Stir in the apple, oil and vanilla extract.

4 Fold the flour mixture into the egg mixture using a large metal spoon, taking care not to over mix.

5 Transfer the cake mixture to the prepared baking tin and bake on the middle shelf of the oven for about 25 minutes, until just firm. To check that the cake is cooked, insert a fine skewer into the centre – it should come out clean.

6 Cool the cake in the tin for 15 minutes, and then cut it into 16 slices.

Top tip Take care when you fold the flour mixture into the wet ingredients, as over mixing can prevent the cake from rising.

APPLE STRUDEL

10½ Points per recipe

Ⓥ Serves 8

Preparation time: 20 minutes

Cooking time: 35–40 minutes

Calories per serving: 100

Freezing: recommended

This is a traditional dessert from Austria and Germany, made with paper thin pastry filled with spiced apples and sultanas.

low fat cooking spray

finely grated zest and juice of 1 lemon

450 g (1 lb) cooking apples

40 g (1½ oz) light muscovado sugar

25 g (1 oz) fresh white breadcrumbs

25 g (1 oz) sultanas

1 teaspoon ground mixed spice

6 sheets filo pastry, defrosted if frozen

2 teaspoons icing sugar, for dusting

1 Preheat the oven to Gas Mark 5/ 190°C/fan oven 170°C. Spray a non stick baking sheet with low fat cooking spray.

2 Put the lemon zest and juice into a large bowl. Peel, core and thinly slice the apples, adding them to the lemon juice as you go, to prevent them from turning brown. Mix the sugar, breadcrumbs, sultanas and mixed spice into the apples.

3 Take 2 sheets of filo pastry and lay them side by side, long sides together. Overlap them by 5 cm (2 inches), and then spray once or twice with low fat cooking spray. Cover with two more sheets, overlapping and spraying as before, and then repeat until all 6 sheets of pastry have been used.

4 Spread the fruit mixture along one long edge of the pastry, fold in the two short sides, and then roll up carefully from the long edge to enclose the fruit. Place it on the prepared baking sheet, curling the strudel to fit, if necessary.

5 Bake for 35–40 minutes, or until the apples are tender and the strudel is golden brown. Cool slightly, and then serve, dusted with the icing sugar.

Top tip Keep the filo pastry covered with a clean, damp tea towel or clingfilm to prevent the sheets from drying out as you work.

Variation Serve the strudel with 1 tablespoon of low fat plain yogurt, adding ½ an extra Point per serving.

RASPBERRY YOGURT MUFFINS

3 POINTS

33¹/₂ Points per recipe

Ⓥ Makes 12

Preparation time: 15 minutes

Cooking time: 15–20 minutes

Calories per muffin: 190

Freezing: recommended

Muffins are a treat that come from the USA, although you might find that they are twice the size on the other side of the Atlantic! We've made these smaller versions to help keep the Points in control.

300 g (10¹/₂ oz) plain white flour
2 teaspoons baking powder
¹/₂ teaspoon ground cinnamon
150 g (5¹/₂ oz) light muscovado sugar
100 g (3¹/₂ oz) fresh raspberries
1 egg
150 g (5¹/₂ oz) low fat plain yogurt
150 ml (5 fl oz) skimmed milk
3 tablespoons sunflower oil

1 Preheat the oven to Gas Mark 6/200°C/fan oven 180°C. Line a 12 hole muffin tray with paper muffin cases, or use squares of greaseproof paper pushed into the holes.

2 Sift the flour, baking powder and cinnamon into a large mixing bowl. Stir in the sugar and raspberries.

3 Beat the egg, yogurt, milk and oil together, and then stir this into the dry ingredients, taking care not to over mix. Spoon the muffin mixture into the paper cases.

4 Bake for 15–20 minutes, until the muffins are risen and golden brown. Cool in the tray for a few minutes, and then transfer the muffins to a wire rack to cool completely.

Top tip The secret of successful muffins is to avoid beating the mixture too much when you add the wet ingredients to the dry ones. They need to be lightly stirred together until just combined.

Variation Use 100 g (3¹/₂ oz) fresh blueberries instead of raspberries. The Points per serving will remain the same.

Raspberry Yogurt Muffins: Ideal with your morning cup of tea for just 3 Points.

A

American apple pie 58
American beefburger 18
apples: American apple pie 58
    apple strudel 62

B

balti, chick pea 37
beef: American beefburger 18
    beef bourguignon 24
    goulash 24
    lasagne 27
brownie cake, chocolate 62

C

cake, chocolate brownie 62
cannelloni, spinach and cheese 41
cherry clafoutis 57
chick pea balti 37
chicken: chicken noodle soup 10
    chicken tikka masala 25
    coq au vin 28
    Jamaican jerk chicken 31
    jambalaya 14
    stir fried chicken 21
chilli prawn kebabs 50
chilli, vegetable 38
chocolate: chocolate brownie cake 62
    chocolate chip cookies 61
    chocolate roulade 59
    pots au chocolat 58
chow mein, vegetable 38
cookies, chocolate chip 61
coq au vin 28
crème caramel 57
curries: chick pea balti 37
    chicken tikka masala 25
    Indian fish curry 49
    lamb rogan josh 23
    Thai fish curry 46
    Thai vegetable curry 19

D

dahl, spinach and potato 35

E

enchiladas, vegetable 41

F

fish: Indian fish curry 49
    salmon en croûte 45
    seafood chowder 8
    seafood provençal 45
    sole florentine 48
    Thai fish cakes 49
    Thai fish curry 46
French onion soup 12

G

garlic prawns 12
gazpacho 8
goulash, Hungarian 24

H

ham and mushroom pizza 17
houmous with pitta 12
Hungarian goulash 24

I

Indian fish curry 49

J

Jamaican jerk chicken 31
jambalaya 14

K

key lime pie 54
kebabs, chilli prawn 50

L

lamb: lamb rogan josh 23
    Moroccan lamb tagine 27
    moussaka 28
    Spanish meatballs 20
lasagne 27
lemon soufflé 61

M

meatballs, Spanish 20
minestrone 11
Moroccan lamb tagine 27
moules marinieres 46
moussaka 28
muffins, raspberry yogurt 63
mushroom pizza, ham and 17
mushroom risotto 39
mussels: moules marinieres 46

N

noodles, teriyuki 18

O

onion soup, French 12

P

paella 42
pasta: pasta primavera 34
    spaghetti bolognese 20
    spinach and cheese cannelloni 41
    tagliatelle carbonara 19
pastries, spinach and feta 37
pavlova, summer 53
pies, sweet: American apple pie 58
    key lime pie 54
    plum tarte tatin 54
pizza, ham and mushroom 17

plum tarte tatin 54
pork: sticky ribs 10
    sweet and sour pork 31
potato dahl, spinach and 35
pots au chocolat 58
prawns: chilli prawn kebabs 50
    garlic prawns 12
    prawn laksa 50

R

raspberry yogurt muffins 63
risotto, mushroom 39
rogan josh, lamb 23
roulade, chocolate 59

S

salmon en croûte 45
samosas, vegetable 13
seafood, mixed: paella 42
    seafood chowder 8
    seafood provençal 45
sole florentine 48
soufflé, lemon 61
soups: chicken noodle soup 10
    French onion soup 12
    gazpacho 8
    minestrone 11
    seafood chowder 8
spaghetti bolognese 20
Spanish meatballs 20
spinach: spinach and cheese cannelloni 41
    spinach and feta pastries 37
    spinach and potato dahl 35
spring rolls, Thai 7
steak au poivre 17
sticky ribs 10
stir fries: stir fried chicken 21
    sweet and sour stir fry 32
summer pavlova 53
sweet and sour pork 31
sweet and sour stir fry 32

T

tagine, Moroccan lamb 27
tagliatelle carbonara 19
tarte tatin, plum 54
teriyaki noodles 18
Thai fish cakes 49
Thai fish curry 46
Thai spring rolls 7
Thai vegetable curry 19
tiramisu with strawberries 57
tortilla chips and dips 11

V

vegetable chilli 38
vegetable chow mein 38
vegetable curry, Thai 19
vegetable enchiladas 41
vegetable samosas 13